Joseph Mitchell

Joseph Mitchell

A Reader's and Writer's Guide

Raymond J. Rundus

iUniverse, Inc.
New York Lincoln Shanghai

Joseph Mitchell
A Reader's and Writer's Guide

iUniverse, Inc.

For information address:
iUniverse
2021 Pine Lake Road, Suite 100
Lincoln, NE 68512
www.iuniverse.com

ISBN: 0-595-28739-5 (Pbk)
ISBN: 0-595-65842-3 (Cloth)

Printed in the United States of America

for all of those—other writers and researchers, colleagues hither, thither, and yon; family members and friends yon, thither and hither; all who have sustained and nourished me—this book, in tribute to and honor of Joseph Quincy Mitchell and all like him, is humbly dedicated

"[The best cooks] have to be old; it takes a lifetime to learn how to do a thing simply." *Old Mr. Flood* (1948)

"A writer doesn't write about what he knows; he writes about what it is that he doesn't know about what he knows." Eudora Welty, in *One Writer's Beginnings*

"At the end of your life, you are the only one who knows how far you fell short of what you intended. And that doesn't help, because at the end of your life you don't always know what you intended." Joseph Mitchell (1992)

"You're still fooling them, aren't you, Daddy?" Nora Mitchell

CONTENTS

FOREWORD

Someone has said that many a letter is written only for the sake of the "Postscript." Glancing at the format of this study of Joseph Mitchell and at its "Table of Contents," a desultory reader may conclude that this book has been written for the sake of the annotated bibliographies that comprise the greater share of its length. There is some truth in this observation.

At least one acquisitions editor whom I queried about publishing an earlier version of this manuscript warned me of the danger of doing what I have now completed doing: writing ever-longer annotations in the bibliography of my work. And in spite of his animadversions, you will find numerous examples of prolixity in what will follow here: divided neatly nonetheless into categories such as primary sources, secondary sources (reviews and criticism), and secondary bibliography (ancillary and corollary sources). The last category may prove to be—even compared to the commentaries I have provided on Mr. Mitchell's primary materials—the most interesting, useful, and "authentic" of what is here offered.

What ensues in this study may seem at times heretical to those who tend to think inside the box or draw within the outlines of the picture. But what fun would that be all the time? And who would ever want to write a book if "fun" wasn't what was wanted or needed? So perhaps I have regressed here somewhat to the mind set of the six-year-old boy who was asked how he created the pictures that he liked to draw. He thought for a bit, and then said, "Well, first I think. And then I draw a line around my think." And so perhaps have I.

Those readers wanting to gain specific information and to understand better and therefore to appreciate more fully the artistry of Joseph Mitchell—this great prose stylist, this subtle and complex rhetorician, this masterful student of human nature—will, if they follow the course of this book carefully and thus well, understand why such diverse observers of Joseph Mitchell's art as Salman Rushdie, Harold Bloom, Allan Gurganus, and Alec Wilkinson have come to believe he has a valid claim to literary immortality.

It may not be too immodest for me to suggest that what I have put into practice in this "Guide" is something like what Stuart Gilbert was doing when he compiled and published his study of the structure and themes of Joyce's *Ulysses*, a text that led Joseph Mitchell to a more intimate understanding of a novel that, as he said, he had read in college and "never got over." Staffers at the

New Yorker (those who knew Joseph Mitchell best both in his temperament and in his craftsmanship) have described this consummate Southerner who became a citizen of the world as "Joyce By the Hudson" and have said of his popular collection of stories, *McSorley's Wonderful Saloon*, that it was "this city's *Dubliners*."

The zest for living, as with much of Joyce, that Joseph Mitchell's characters exhibit (many of whom, if not most, while struggling to survive or confronting an ultimately uncertain destiny, and who face that destiny with only their faith in the value of living and their knowing how to make a livelihood to sustain them) is his one transcendent theme. The characters is his stories are nearly all men, and nearly all of them have worked hard all their lives (Joe Gould being the apparent—but only apparent—exception) in occupations related to providing for others as for themselves the basics of human existence: food, clothing, shelter, and most importantly, a strong sense of self manifested and exhibited within a particular community.

Joseph Mitchell's "graveyard humor" is exemplified in a country saying that stayed in his psyche throughout his 87-plus years: "From the cradle to the hearse,/Things aren't so bad that they can't be worse." And in another succinct expression of a homely philosophy, he told David Streitfeld in 1992, "Life's a goddam mess, but you wouldn't want to miss it."

What you will find here then is a "Guide" to a rich life, discovered both in the art of a great reporter and writer (whose listening skills were exemplary and legendary) and in the variety and extent of the friendships and allegiances that illustrate, define, and justify the scope and ultimate worth of Joseph Mitchell's life: among them assuredly both his intimate involvement in institutions (from the First Baptist Church of Fairmont to Grace [Episcopal] Church in Manhattan) and his many commitments to public service (from being a "Friend of Cast-Iron Architecture" to joining the British Gypsy Lore Society to accepting an appointment by Mayor Ed Koch to the Landmarks Preservation Commission). Most importantly to him at the end of his life, no doubt, were the relationships and friendships that sustained, motivated, added depth of meaning to his day-to-day activities, and gave more authenticity to both himself and to those privileged to have claims upon his attention, interest, and love: from street people like Joe Gould and the Reverend Hall to sidewalk habitués, barflies, saloon philosophers and business proprietors (like Mazie P. Gordon, Tim Costello, John McSorley, Max Gordon, Louis Morino and the "Don't Swear Man,"); freaks and eccentrics and anomalies (like the bearded "Lady Olga," fan and bubble dancers and nudists, Philippa Duke Schuyler [a mixed-race child with a certified I.Q. of 185]; a married couple residing in a cave in Central Park; Commodore Dutch aka "The Tooth"; "Santa Claus Smith"; "conjure woman"

Marie Leveau; and Cockeye Johnny Nikanov); and what would seem like (in reviewing his nine years as a newspaper reporter in New York) a cast of thousands of "celebrities of the day": Kate Smith, Jimmy Durante, Eleanor Roosevelt, George Bernard Shaw, Billy Sunday, William Steig, George M. Cohan, Franz Boas, Fats Waller, Rudy Vallee, and Clara Bow are but a few examples. When he was assigned to cover the Lindbergh kidnapping trial, Joseph Mitchell thought of this out-of-town assignment as a vacation.

And then there were photographers that he came to know or know the work of, such as his wife Therese, Walker Evans, Berenice Abbott, Diane Arbus, and Anne Hall. And, among the artists at the *New Yorker* (Ross's insistence that the cartoonists be always called "artists" persists to this day): Charles Addams and Saul Steinberg, the latter having done the drawings for *The Bottom of the Harbor*. But perhaps ultimately, since his fame and reputation rest upon his becoming a veritable icon in the writing fraternity, there were—and remain— and have continued to expand even after his death in 1996—his connections to writers and editors, such as Stanley Walker, St. Clair McKelway, E. B. and Katharine (Angell) White, William Maxwell, Roger Angell, Charles ("Chip") McGrath, James Thurber, Howard Nemerov, Stanley Edgar Hyman and Shirley Jackson, and Marie Winn; *New Yorker* editors-in-chief Harold Ross, William Shawn, Robert Gottlieb, and Tina Brown; female staffers or contributors like Lillian Ross, Jean Stafford, Janet Malcolm, Nancy Franklin, and Mindy Aloff; old timers, nearly also all who could be called "cronies"—and whom he mostly admired—like S. J. Perelman, G. T. Ryall ("Audax Minor"), Emily Hahn, Philip Hamburger, and Brendan Gill.

None was as important to him as his friendship (Mitchell said it was based on "literary argument," such as whether Marlow or Shakespeare was the better writer) with Abbott Joseph ("Joe" or "A. J.") Liebling, who became such a close friend that he and his third wife Jean Stafford moved in the fall of 1961 to 45 West 10th Street in Greenwich Village, directly across the street from the Mitchells, who had been the only witnesses at their wedding.

Among a more contemporary generation there are *New Yorker* staff writers like Mark Singer, Alec Wilkinson, and Calvin Trillin. And most importantly to him in his last few years was Sheila McGrath, a Canadian native who had been an administrative assistant to William Shawn and in the course of time became Mr. Mitchell's caretaker, confidante, literary assistant, companion, executrix of his literary estate, and equal heir along with daughters Nora and Elizabeth to his considerable land holdings in Robeson County.

It has become—over the past year or so and in the process of intellectual evolution—the purpose of this "Guide," then, to attempt to bring forth and put in swaddling clothes the diverse and rich life of Joseph Quincy Mitchell

(1908-1996): as an interviewer or interlocutor, a writer, a colleague, a mentor, and a friend. As his editor at Random House for the Modern Library series, Susan DiSesa, said to me of Mr. Mitchell, "He has given so much." This study, then, if it is successful, will illustrate how much of himself—his knowledge, talent, temperament, and craftsmanship—Joseph Mitchell has so far left to us.

CHRONOLOGY

(* identifies a topic dealt with in one of the author's writings)

1889 *Joseph Ferdinand Gould born September 12 in Norwood, Massachusetts.

1908 Joseph Quincy Mitchell born near Fairmont, NC, July 17, the eldest of the three sons and three daughters of Averette Nance ("A. N.") and Elizabeth Amanda (Parker) Mitchell. His middle name is derived from his grandfather, Quince Bostic Mitchell (1852-1896).

1925 Enrolls at the University of North Carolina at Chapel Hill where he stays for four years but leaves in 1929 without a degree.

1929 Arrives in New York from North Carolina at Pennsylvania Station on Friday, October 25, four days before the great stock market crash. (An error often found in writings about Mitchell's arrival has the market crashing on Thursday, October 24; but "Black Tuesday" was October 29, 1929.) Begins work as a reporter for the *New York World*.

1930 Works for *New York Herald Tribune* until fired in 1931.

1931 Works for three months as seaman or "deck boy" on a freighter shipping between New York and Leningrad. Marries Therese Dagny Engelsted Jacobsen February 27. Begins work as a reporter for *New York World Telegram*—meets A. J. Liebling.

1933 Publishes first signed piece in *NY*, November 11 issue.

1938 Becomes a staff writer on September 26 at *NY*, joining A. J. Liebling. Publishes *My Ears Are Bent*, a collection of his *World Telegram* pieces.

1943 Publishes *McSorley's Wonderful Saloon*. Malcolm Cowley writes first essay to claim that Mitchell is a writer of literary significance.

1948 Publishes *Old Mr. Flood*, which the author describes as stories that "are truthful rather than factual, but they are solidly based on facts."

1957 Death of *Joe Gould on August 18, less than one month shy of his 68th birthday. A funeral service is held nine days later in New York City.

1960 Publishes *The Bottom of the Harbor* and the lead essay, "Mohawks in High Steel," in Edmund Wilson's *Apologies to the Iroquois*.

1963 Death on December 28 of A. J. Liebling; Mitchell delivers his eulogy at the memorial service two days later.

1964 *Bajour*, a musical based on Mitchell's Gypsy stories, begins a Broadway run that lasts for 232 performances. His two-part series, "Joe Gould's Secret," is published in the *New Yorker*, his last contribution to that magazine.'

1965 Publishes *Joe Gould's Secret*, his last publication until 1992.

1972 Begins eight years of service as a charter member of South Street Seaport Museum as a member of the Restoration Committee.

1980 Death of Therese Mitchell in Fairmont on October 22. Burial in Floyd Family Cemetery in Fairmont.

1982 Begins period of five years' service on New York Landmarks Preservation Commission.

1984 Receives North Carolina Award in Literature in Raleigh, North Carolina.

1992 Pantheon publishes *Up in the Old Hotel and Other Stories*, collecting all of Mitchell's previously published work (except for *My Ears Are Bent*) and adding seven previously unpublished short stories.

1993 One of eight recipients of the University of North Carolina at Chapel Hill's Distinguished Alumnus Award during the University's Bicentennial. *Up in the Old Hotel* wins both the Brendan Gill Prize from the Municipal Art Society and (in the category of "American Arts and Letters") the Ambassador Book Award from the English-Speaking Union.

1994 *The Bottom of the Harbor* reissued in the new "Modern Library" series.

1996 *Joe Gould's Secret* reissued in the new "Modern Library" series. On February 6 Mitchell does his first—and last—public reading, from the 1964 profile of Joe Gould. Dies at age 87 on May 24 in a New York hospital and is buried in the Floyd Family Cemetery in Fairmont beside Therese. A "Postscript" feature in *NY* features tributes from the editors and writers at the magazine. On October 2, a "Tribute" service is held at the Century Club; those participating are Tina Brown, Brendan Gill, Susan di Sesa (his "Modern Library" editor), William Maxwell (who reads from "Mazie"), and Philip Hamburger.

1997 Posthumously inducted on May 17 into the North Carolina Literary Hall of Fame.

2000 The movie version of *Joe Gould's Secret* opens nationally on April 7 and is shown in five New York theaters. Released on videotape September 26. Celebrating the magazine's seventy-fifth anniversary, The New Yorker Festival on May 6 offers a round table discussion of "The life and work of Joseph Mitchell," moderated by Dan Frank and with Nancy Franklin, Stanley Tucci, Philip Hamburger, and Alec Wilkinson.

2001 Both *My Ears Are Bent* and *McSorley's Wonderful Saloon* are reissued in the summer by Pantheon in handsome new editions. Eli Wallach and Calvin Trillin read from *MWS* in McSorley's Old Ale House. Hijacked jet-liners on Tuesday, September 11, destroy both the North and South Towers of the World Trade Center in Lower Manhattan, both altering forever the destiny of the United States and putting closure to a "lost world":

the arena of human lives and institutions which Joseph Mitchell and A. J. Liebling explored and celebrated.

LIST OF ABBREVIATIONS

Apologies = Apologies to the Iroquois (1960)

Bottom = The Bottom of the Harbor ([1960], 1994: in "Modern Library" reprint)

Ears = My Ears Are Bent (1938: Pantheon revised and amplified edition in 2001)

Flood = Old Mr. Flood (1948: admitted by Mitchell in 1992 to be fictional—and thus a "novel")

JGS = Joe Gould's Secret (1965 ["Modern Library" reprint in 1996, other American editions in 1996, 1999, 2000])

MWS = McSorley's Wonderful Saloon (1943, Pantheon revised and amplified edition in 2001)

"Mohawks" = "The Mohawks in High Steel" (1949, rpt. in *Apologies* in 1960)

NY = The New Yorker

Up = Up in the Old Hotel (1992)

INTRODUCTION

Elated after being told in the summer of 1929 by his father, Averette Nance Mitchell, that he would not have to return to the University of North Carolina at Chapel Hill so as to satisfy the math and chemistry requirements keeping him from graduating, Joseph Quincy Mitchell set his sights on moving from his hometown of Fairmont to New York City, with the aim of becoming a political reporter.

He soon found work on the *New York World* and a short while later as a "district man" with the more prestigious *Herald Tribune*, from which he was four months later fired for an act of youthful insubordination. Confessing himself sick of the burdens of witnessing, reporting, and writing about the tawdry and brutal side of life, he broke entirely with his past and went to sea, serving a tour of duty as a mariner for several months on a transoceanic freighter shipping pulp logs from Russia. He returned to Manhattan to marry Therese Dagny Engelsted Jacobsen, a photographer, and to continue newspaper work at the *New York World-Telegram*. He soon became the paper's star reporter, and his articles were heralded on its delivery trucks. A few months before he reported for work in September 1938 at *The New Yorker* (to which he had been contributing articles since 1933), he published his first book, *My Ears Are Bent*, a collection of his newspaper pieces, which began with a gritty, breezy, and remarkably candid autobiographical essay, also titled "My Ears Are Bent."

Joseph Mitchell's long career (an association of 63 years) at *The New Yorker*—though he did not publish anything in the magazine after 1964 (the two-part series titled "Joe Gould's Secret")—ended with his death in 1996. This two-part profile was published together with his 1942 profile of Gould ("Professor Sea Gull") to make up his 1965 book *Joe Gould's Secret*.

As he prepared with Dan Frank, his editor at Pantheon, and with Sheila McGrath, his longtime companion and literary assistant, for the publication of his 1992 anthology, *Up in the Old Hotel*, Mr. Mitchell decided to return "Professor Sea Gull" to its original place in his 1943 collection, *McSorley's Wonderful Saloon*. He also decided not to include *My Ears Are Bent* in this anthology, believing that it was writing of another kind. But he did add five new nonfiction pieces and two new fiction pieces (all of these also first appearing in *NY*) to the "McSorley's Wonderful Saloon" section. He now also openly admitted that his 1948 book, *Old Mr. Flood* (originally three separate pieces in

NY) was fictional, and thus in actuality a novel. The last book he and Dan Frank included, *The Bottom of the Harbor* (1960), six "stories" about and around New York Harbor, is considered to be his richest and most mature work. *Joe Gould's Secret* (made into a fine film adaptation in 2000) offers, however, the intrigue of a great and unsolved and seemingly unsolvable mystery: why a writer of Joseph Mitchell's stature and achievements would make this his last published work, lapsing into a puzzling and profound silence after he unburdened himself of the guilt and shame he had suffered when he became aware that he had been taken in by the writer of "The Oral History of the World," Joseph Ferdinand Gould, of whom, he ultimately said, "I became him and he became me, if you see what I mean."

At the funeral services in 1963 for A. J. Liebling, his best friend on both the *World-Telegram* and *NY* and at his death his near neighbor in Greenwich Village, Joseph Mitchell said this: "In other words, what I am getting at, Joe is dead, but he really isn't. He is dead, but he will live again. Every time anyone anywhere in all the years to come takes down one of his books and read or rereads one of his wonderful stories, he will live again" (Qtd. in Sokolov, *Wayward Reporter*, 322). The same will and must and even more aptly can be said for Joseph Mitchell. *Up in the Old Hotel* remains in print, still selling thousands of copies a year. The 1938 edition of *My Ears Are Bent* (a handsome new edition came out from Pantheon in 2001) is avidly sought and, even if a copy is miraculously located, will require an outlay of $400 to $500 for even a discarded library book and well into four figures for other volumes.

By the time he died in May 1996, Joseph Mitchell had earned unprecedented admiration and respect from the editors and his fellow writers at *NY*, as witness the unique "Postscript" tribute to him in that magazine in its June 10 issue. His international reputation has continued to grow, with translations being made and praises being offered for his achievements: from such admirers and observers as Doris Lessing, Julian Barnes, John Fowles, Martin Amis, and Salman Rushdie. He also is remembered for serving the city of New York in several important posts: being appointed by Mayor Koch as a Commissioner for Landmarks Preservation, being a key member of the South Street Seaport Museum board, becoming a member of the Society of Architectural Historians and of the Society of Industrial Archeology, and one of the Friends of Cast-Iron Architecture. More personal interests and involvements include his service as vestryman to Grace Church, which, though Episcopal in denomination and thus quite remote from the two Protestant denominations he knew from youth, may have been his favorite New York institution. He also was a longtime and active member of the James Joyce Society, the Century Club, and the Gypsy Lore Society of Great Britain. As an officer of the Institute and Academy of

American Arts and Letters, he moved among a virtual pantheon of American literary lights. But, in contrast, he was also a member of a much more intimate group, the "Deep Six," which was founded by Harvey Orkin, included among others S. J Perelman and Al Hirschfeld, and met weekly until Orkin's passing.

His two favorite authors were James Joyce (his beloved "JJ") and Mark Twain, but he and A. J. Liebling both admired and were influenced by the more than three-hundred-year history of literary journalism, from Daniel Defoe through Henry Fielding and especially by the nineteenth century realistic non-fiction writers *cum* journalists: William Cobbett, George Borrow, and Pierce Egan the elder. Stephen Crane was also a favorite of both, though Liebling gained more from his writing. Joseph Mitchell also admired the poetry of Elizabeth Bishop, the writing about food (he was the office authority on fish and seafood at *NY*) of M. F. K. Fisher and the poetry of fellow North Carolinian A. R. Ammons, the creative works of Dickens, Dostoevsky, Gogol, Turgenev, Breughel, Matisse, and Heywood C. Broun (he made Broun also a favorite of "Old Mr. Flood"), the Old Testament, especially "Proverbs" and "Ecclesiastes," jazz music, and so on. Among his friends at *NY*, in addition to A. J. Liebling, one would have to mention Perelman, the artist Saul Steinberg, William Maxwell, Stanley Edgar Hyman and his wife Shirley Jackson, Philip Hamburger, Nancy Franklin, Janet Malcolm, Roger Angell, Mark Singer, Calvin Trillin, Brendan Gill, Alec Wilkinson, Mindy Aloff, and many others, those much younger than he as well as several who were his contemporaries. He knew and appreciated the contributions that E. B. White and James Thurber had made to the magazine, but Thurber was closer to his own spirit. Other relationships of importance would include the poet Howard Nemerov and Diane Arbus (Nemerov's photographer sister), Jean Stafford (ultimately Liebling's third wife), Susan DiSesa (his editor at Modern Library), Peter De Vries, Tim Costello (co-owner of Costello's Bar—a favorite *NY* watering hole), Lillian Ross, St. Clair McKelway and Katharine (Angell) White (his earliest editors at the magazine), and Stanley Walker, the city editor of the *Herald Tribune* who was his first contact in New York and who gave him invaluable early advice. Among the women with whom he became good friends in his later years were Sheila McGrath, a former office assistant to William Shawn at *NY* (and later his companion, literary assistant, and heiress) and Marie Winn, an emigrée from "Cold War" Europe who had become a successful writer (*The Plug-In Drug*) in this country.

The forthcoming biography of Joseph Mitchell by Thomas Kunkel (who wrote the superb, Pulitzer-Prize nominated 1995 biography of Harold Ross, *Genius in Disguise*) will, by examining Joseph Mitchell's many and fruitful friendships and allegiances and by laying out the significance of his diverse and many interests and commitments, bring forward an authentic, compelling portrait of a man in full. He was after all not only the consummate Southern gentleman, but, paradoxically it might seem, the consummate literary historian of Manhattan (one prominent observer called him "Joyce by the Hudson") of the past century and perhaps that century's greatest artist/reporter, a sophisticated citizen of the world—and one of the writers of the past century who will continue to be read and reread, world without end.

The horrifying events of Tuesday, September 11, 2001 (nearly 72 years after the "Black Tuesday" that marked Joseph Mitchell's first visit to Lower Manhattan) have served to enhance and somehow make more noble the characters he portrayed always as communal beings, men and women who, by finding meaning and vitality among their fellows, managed to authenticate their own existence. The social history of New York would be sorely diminished without his finely etched profiles of such mythomaniacs as Bowery philanthropist Mazie P. Gordon, "King of the Gypsies" Cockeye Johnny Nikanov, Jane Barnell (the bearded "Lady Olga"), the Mohawk Indian construction workers of Brooklyn, the child genius Philippa Duke Schuyler (who would die heroically and tragically in Vietnam), George Hunter (the most admirable of his characters), Dragger Captain Ellery Thompson, street preacher the Reverend Mr. James Jefferson Davis Hall, the Norway rats on the New York Harbor waterfront, and Joseph Ferdinand Gould, the unsinkable "Professor Sea Gull."

The annotated bibliography which follows will be useful to scholars and researchers. More importantly because more enduringly, its larger reach brings the personality and character of Joseph Mitchell more intimately into the intellectual and spiritual lives of his readers and admirers.

*   *   *   *   *

A Special Note on Joseph Mitchell's Thematic Values and His Style

In his 1993 study of Joseph Mitchell in *Pembroke Magazine 26*, Sanford Smoller observed that Mitchell (whom Clifton Fadiman in 1938 had described as an "angel of the odd" and "imp of the perverse") in his mature work exhibited six enduring values, all of these being subsidiary to the tension that transcends his art: the "opposition of health, goodness, and life to sickness, evil, and death." His characters, Smoller says, appeal to us because (emphases mine)

(1) they *resist the evils* brought upon human lives by the "pressures and infringements of a relentlessly conformist mechanistic society"; (2) they *refuse to bow to adversity* no matter how seemingly marginal their social standing or income; (3) they *know how to have a good time*, particularly as that good time involves eating as well as possible; (4) they *want to live as long as possible*, for a long life exhibits lyric, even elegiac, nobility; (5) because their lives privilege *the nostalgia of history and the poignancy of tradition*, the artifacts they seek in order to make a living become urges more worthy in their psyches than the grim sensory details of the modern wasteland; and (6) the great dilemma which finally erupted from Mitchell's personal relationship with Joe Gould, a fellow, conflicted writer: *does the writer have the moral right to use people for his own purpose and then discard them when they are no longer useful to him?* When Mitchell himself had to face this dilemma, Smoller suggests, he was unable to find an answer that he could live with for the rest of his life—and thus he chose not to make a choice, and—at least for publication—he ceased to write.

In Joseph Mitchell's hometown of Fairmont ("Stonewall" in his fiction) the First Baptist Church is sited at the east end of Church Street. For most of his formative years and always in his adult life, 305 Church Street—just two blocks up the street—was his "home." First Baptist Church was the church of his father, Averette Nance Mitchell (familiarly known as "A. N."). At Joseph Mitchell's burial in Fairmont in the Floyd Family Cemetery, the pastor emeritus of this church read the eulogy for Fairmont's most famous native son. Across from this church is its small, now outgrown graveyard, not as imposing as the one in Iona Presbyterian Church, a few miles from Fairmont and the home church of his mother, Elizabeth Amanda Parker Mitchell. Sunday afternoon visits to this latter graveyard Joseph Mitchell has described memorably in the "Author's Note" to *Up in the Old Hotel* as having had a profound effect on the development of his most prominent cast of mind, which he described as "graveyard humor."

But that *other* graveyard also had a share in the development of his prominent cast of mind. In 1989, in an interview in his *New Yorker* office with Norman Sims, in which he spoke openly for the first time in over two decades about his writing, Michell recalled an Easter-egg hunt he took part in that was sponsored by the Sunday school teachers for their charges. But first some family background.

Joseph Mitchell's middle name, Quincy, derived from his grandfather, Quince Bostic Mitchell (1852-1896), who was buried in the First Baptist Church cemetery along with other of the Mitchell forebears. Quince Bostic Mitchell's grave today and the grave of his wife and Joseph's grandmother,

Catherine Rebecca Mitchell (1859-1924), are marked by a handsome white stone.

As Mr. Mitchell described to Sims his search for Easter eggs hidden among the gravestones, he recalled finding under some dead leaves on his grandfather's grave a robin's-egg-blue egg. To him in later years the symbolic or archetypal significance of this event was powerful, one of the shaping elements of his outlook on life. It is found in the sermon of the old Negro street preacher in the reverie passage in *Joe Gould's Secret*, who speaks of the seeds of pomegranates and of eggs all standing for the Resurrection. Graveyards or cemeteries and burials in the earth or in the water—as an apparent consequence of these early shaping experiences—have come to figure prominently in a number of Joseph Mitchell's most memorable narratives, such as "Mr. Hunter's Grave," "The Rivermen," and "The Bottom of the Harbor."

To Malcolm Jones of *Newsweek* (who wrote about Joseph Mitchell in 1992 and again in 2001 after the republication of *My Ears Are Bent* and *McSorley's Wonderful Saloon*), Joseph Mitchell's philosophy of life was summed up in an old country saying that he shared with Jones: "From the cradle to the hearse, things aren't so bad that they can't get worse."

In his early adult life Mr. Mitchell was to come across the sketches of a Mexican street artist, José Guadalupe Posada, whose *calaveras*, scenes of life in which the animate figures are depicted as skeletons, became the graphic complement to his descriptions in print of such scenes. Mitchell was first introduced to Posada as a printmaker in 1933 by *Frida Kahlo, whom he was sent to interview at her hotel by his editors at the *World-Telegram*. He came to admire and greatly respect Posada, this proletarian street artist, and he looked for books by and about him whenever the opportunity arose. The latent humor in the scenes of skeletons dancing a fandango, of well-known contemporary and historical figures in skeleton guise performing their traditional roles in life, amused the writer and deeply affected his literary point of view.

For a long time at *NY*, neophyte contributors were given copies of articles by Joseph Mitchell with this admonition: "Read the Master." And at some time toward the end of Joseph Mitchell's active career at *NY*, a teacher at City College of New York, according to Calvin Trillin, would refer to Mitchell as the "greatest living master of the English declarative sentence." One suspects this teacher may have been Trillin's late wife, Alice, who taught at CCNY for a number of years and who resorted to photocopying Mitchell's articles en masse for the benefit of her students. Calvin Trillin came to believe that this encomium—whatever its source—became something like an albatross around Mitchell's neck, and that a primary reason for his ceasing to write for publication was his feeling that he was not able to exceed the perfection he had putatively attained.

Be that as it may—and it also may not be—there is little doubt that Joseph Mitchell was a paragon among reporters, exhibiting, as Noel Perrin pointed out in *Sewanee Review* in 1983, a style that "is fast-paced, personal, and deadpan.... All is motion." Calvin Trillin described him, in the dedication to his book *Killings*, as the *NY* writer who "set the standard." And to me as well as to John Boe in *Writing on the Edge*, Trillin said that he "thought that the stuff he wrote for the *New Yorker* was the best of that sort of writing for clarity and simplicity. Somehow he was able to take the marks of writing off the writing; it's almost as if it just appeared on the page." This kind of esteem came about largely because Mitchell was a master of diverse rhetorical strategies, most found within his sentences. The six stories in *The Bottom of the Harbor* are the best places to look for evidence of his mastery of the declarative sentence. The devices or tropes that he wielded especially well are similes and metaphors, the catalogue, parallelism, the balanced sentence—in which the main parts work with (in synthesis) or against (in antithesis) each other, with the middle acting a kind of fulcrum—and the periodic sentence, in which the primary emphasis is anticipated but delayed until the sentence's end. Alec Wilkinson, in his 1992 *Vogue* essay about Joseph Mitchell, "Setting the Standard," described the style of this master's prose memorably and accurately:

> A Mitchell sentence is sleek, graceful, and rambunctious. It is never rushed, it never contains unnecessary or inexact words, it is never flamboyant or self-promoting, and its rhythm is always solid, musical, and distinct. His pieces are meticulous in their construction yet have no suggestion of artifice. They are layered and deep and full of resonance, so that a person can read them again and again and again and feel each time as if he has come away with something he may not have realized was present before. I have read his books so often that I have unintentionally memorized parts of them, but I don't ever feel that I've come to the end of Joseph Mitchell.

It should be added that Alec Wilkinson told me in 1995 that he was more of a rereader than a reader, and, having much of Joseph Mitchell by heart, he would even want to read his laundry list.

Describing and analyzing the sentences of a craftsman like Joseph Mitchell can be readily practiced by students, teachers, amateur grammarians, and practicing rhetoricians in nearly anything and in almost everything that Joseph Mitchell ever wrote: they will therefore not need, in this brief introduction to the themes and rhetoric of his style, a demonstration of the mechanics of his writing.

Joseph Mitchell's *similes and metaphors* will most often remind the reader of similar effects in the writings of George Orwell, the nonfiction writer, who wrote, for example, that the jargon of politicians and sociologists obstructed meaning in the same way tea leaves clogged up a sink. Mitchell's introduction to *Ears*, "My Ears Are Bent," often exhibits such figurative language. And similes taken from ordinary life seem to have come naturally to him. In a telephone conversation we had in late 1994, he complained about being so preoccupied that he felt "like a washing machine." Two of his most memorable similes occur in a story titled "Obituary of a Gin Mill," his first "Reporter at Large" piece to appear in *NY* after he first reported there for work: on September 26, 1938. Dick, the owner of the bar, used to have, before he gentrified his establishment, "the aplomb of a sow on her belly in a bog," but now that his place is as "shiny and undistinguished as a two-dollar alarm clock," he is increasingly nervous and anxious, becoming one of the very few characters in Mitchell's writings who exhibit apprehension.

The use of the *catalogue* is the most common and perhaps the most effective rhetorical device in Joseph Mitchell's repertoire, serving to establish both credulity and certitude as one concrete detail is amassed after another, this sort of thing contributing to the total effect in Joseph Mitchell's writing of a many-layered narrative, of what William Zinsser has referred to as his "mosaicism." Such detail also corroborates Noel Perrin's observation that Joseph Mitchell likely knew more than anyone else did or could about the subjects he wrote about. Examples of the *catalogue* may be found in such disparate pieces as "Evening With a Gifted Child," "King of the Gypsies," *Old Mr. Flood*, and "The Rats on the Waterfront." In the lead story in *The Bottom of the Harbor*, "Up in the Old Hotel," Mitchell and Louis ("Louie") Morino surrender their fears to the powerful urges of curiosity and take an old, creaky, hand-operated elevator to the upper (third to sixth floors) stories of the building, formerly the Fulton Ferry Hotel, in which Louie and his brother Amil operate on the ground floor their restaurant, "Sloppy Louie's." Expecting to find perhaps some old hotel registers or some other relics of value, instead they find such items as these on a marble-top table: "…three seltzer bottles with corroded spouts, a tin water cooler painted to resemble brown marble, a cracked glass bell of the kind used to cover clocks and stuffed birds, and four sugar bowls whose metal flap lids had been eaten away from their hinges by rust."

The use of *parallelism* is illustrated in Joseph Mitchell's prose style most often by his use of a series of adjectives in his description of a person or a scene. This pattern is found everywhere in his *NY* "Profiles" and "Reporter at

Large" stories, from those early pieces collected in *McSorley's Wonderful Saloon* to *Joe Gould's Secret*. Here is an example from "Thirty-two Rats from Casablanca" (later titled "The Rats on the Waterfront") as Mitchell describes the physical characteristics of the brown rat, or *Rattus norvegicus*: "Its nose is blunt, and its ears are small and alert, and its eyes are sharp and shiny and joyless and resentful and accusing." Such a sentence is distinctive to Joseph Mitchell and would by experienced readers be immediately identified—even if the content were changed and only the structure remained—as his and his alone.

It is also worth examining here—even if briefly—the elements of Joseph Mitchell's style—its thematic interest and rhetorical thrust—that extend beyond the level of the sentence. Two observers who are most keen on the Mitchellian style are Luc Sante and William Zinsser.

Sante, who wrote an exemplary review of *Up in the Old Hotel* in the October 5, 1992, issue of *The New Republic*, had come to his admiration of Joseph Mitchell's work only six years before and that by accident. He had in fact assumed, since he had heard nothing previously about him before acquiring a copy of *MWS*, that Mitchell must already be dead. But he came to believe that this writer, who was "unreservedly generous," belonged at least in his own personal pantheon:

> There is his ability to convey masses of learning and lore offhandedly, by a kind of osmosis, while the reader's attention is diverted. There is his control of narrative dynamics, which allows him to balance a casual, almost conversational tone across dramatic ellipses through to clipped endings. And there is his humor, which is not always immediately apparent but is always there, lurking behind even, maybe especially, his grimmest and most melancholy passages—"graveyard humor," he calls it in a prefatory note, citing *Finnegans Wake* and the engravings of Posada, initially surprising choices that make increasing sense in the light of his work's course.

In his 1992 *American Scholar* essay, William Zinsser, among the most respected and influential of contemporary American rhetoricians, described Mitchell's mixture of themes in *Bottom* to be uniquely his own: "...specialized knowledge, pride of labor, enjoyment of the simple pleasures of the present, and mindfulness of the past and the soon-to-be-joined dead." These themes are also found (in less elegiac mode) in *MWS* and *Flood* and in tragic mode in *JGS*. But some more particular organizational devices should be described before we return to a consideration of theme.

Joseph Mitchell's use of *hooks* (sometimes as the result of deploying *equivocal leads*) allowed him to grab his readers by the lapels of their curiosity, insistently pulling them into the world of his stories. This technique in his mature writing became an essential and distinctive feature. In three of the stories in *The Bottom of the Harbor*, "Up in the Old Hotel," "Mr. Hunter's Grave," and "The Rivermen," the narrator-author uses similar strategies to draw his reader into the story. As he told Norman Sims in a statement Sims quotes in his introduction to his and Mark Kramer's anthology, *Literary Journalism* (1995), "You want to take the reader to the last sentence.... I've been after telling a story [i.e., a nonfiction narrative] perhaps with the same structure the fiction writer uses."

These *hooks* are both palpable and seductive. In "Up in the Old Hotel" the narrator wants to rid his mind of "thoughts of death and doom," in "Mr. Hunter's Grave" he heads to the South Shore of Staten Island "when things get too much for me," and in "The Rivermen," he explains what it is that draws him irresistibly, mystically, to the banks of the Hudson River. Each of these beginnings—in compelling but almost subliminal fashion—invites the reader, by going with him on an adventure that awaits us all, to imbibe the elixir of living to the utmost: in the journey with Louis Morino to the upper stories of the Fulton Ferry Hotel, in conversation with the remarkable George H. Hunter and visits with him to the church cemetery he cares for, and in the conversations with Harry Lyons and his friends aboard Harry's shad fishing barge—drinking beer, looking at old photos, worrying among themselves about the purpose of life, and listening to the rope-jumping songs of schoolgirls.

Finally, one cannot become a reader of Joseph Mitchell—or a writer about him—without being prepared to respond, at least on an intuitive (if not cognitive) level, to his deeper reach: into the subconscious of his characters—and, yes, into himself. In his later years, as he reread and reflected upon the meaning and significance of what he had created, he became ever more prepared to accept, even relish, these more profound and mysterious and archetypal and ultimately therefore more stirring dimensions in his writings. A friend of his at *NY*, Stanley Edgar Hyman, as a literary critic had opened the door to such interpretations as early as 1965, coincidentally the year that Mitchell had published his last book and ceased writing for publication.

Although Malcolm Cowley had, in a 1943 review of *MWS* in *New Republic*, first brought attention from the literary and intellectual world to Mitchell as a writer of significance to American and world literature, Hyman, in "The Art of Joseph Mitchell" in *The New Leader* of December 6, 1965, was the first critic to assert the universality of meaning and value in Joseph Mitchell's writings, especially in *The Bottom of the Harbor* and *Joe Gould's Secret*. As early as 1938 in *My Ears Are Bent*, Mitchell was already demonstrating "his gift of perfect pitch for human speech" and at times (as in his profile of the aging evangelist Billy Sunday) "the complex richness" of his later work. He was also able, Hyman says, to reshape at *NY* the traditional protocols of both the "Profile" and Reporter at Large" forms into "supple and poetic instruments for his own special purposes, blending the symbolic and poetic elements of his early fiction with the objectivity and detail of his newspaper reporting," seen already in his expression of mythic and archetypal themes and characters in *MWS*. Hyman boldly asserts that Mitchell is "a formidable prose stylist and a master rhetorician...." But he also finds, beginning with *Old Mr. Flood,* archetypal and symbolic value in his work: the privileging of human dignity, an "Edenic image of the good old days," fertility and resurrection (as seen especially in Mr. Flood's "Damn your doctor!" monologue), and the depths of the unconscious, "most boldly imaged in *The Bottom of the Harbor."*

Hyman's most penetrating and valuable analysis is reserved for *Joe Gould's Secret,* which might appear superficially to be only a "comic portrait of an eccentric" but which ultimately becomes a "pathetic and moving account of a 'lost soul' who had been an unloved boy"—in literary terms a "Jamesian story of life's necessary illusion" and in even deeper terms a "masking (and finally an unmasking) for Mitchell himself." Gould himself becomes "an archetype of Ishmael...a paradigm of alienated man" and finally serves as a metaphor for all of mankind: "Joe Gould's secret, which is the burden of Joseph Mitchell's powerful art, is ultimately the secret of our brief lonely existence on a disinterested planet."

There has always been a great cautionary wisdom behind Alexander Pope's iambic pentameter couplets in *Essay on Criticism*:

> A little learning is a dangerous thing;
> Drink deep, or taste not the Pierian spring:
> There shallow draughts intoxicate the brain,
> And drinking largely sobers us again.

It is certainly as dangerous for the literary critic to dabble in psychiatry (let alone psychoanalysis) as it is for the psychiatrist or psychoanalyst to muddle around in literary theory and interpretation. I therefore would suggest that it would be a mistake to try sorting out the archetypal and symbolic levels of Joseph Mitchell's art without some knowledge and preparation, and that preparation ought to be in the writings and psychiatric practice of Carl Gustav Jung rather than in those of Sigmund Freud or other psychiatrists of more recent vintage.

The reason for this is relatively simple: a Jungian interpretation will lead the reader into the transcendent archetypes of both the collective and individual unconscious (as revealed in the universal experiences found in dreams, myths, fables, fairy tales, and great literature), archetypes which ultimately will lead us to a richer understanding—in the artistry as reportage of Joseph Mitchell—of what Jung believed to be the basic heroic quest of all mankind: for each of us to authenticate the value of our distinctive existence by differentiating our psychic selves from parent and sibling, peer and superior, friend and foe. And that understanding alone will lead us to a richer, more complete understanding of the narratives of Joseph Mitchell.

Bibliography of Primary Sources

NOTE: Except for those pieces he himself collected and published in *My Ears Are Bent* (1938), it has proven impossible to track down newspaper stories that Joseph Mitchell wrote during his nine years or so in the newspaper business with the *New York World*, the *New York Herald Tribune* or the *New York World-Telegram*. In 1967 the picture files from the *World-Telegram*—and in its other incarnations the *World-Telegram and Sun* and finally the *World Journal Tribune*—were donated to the Library of Congress. This archival material, covering the period from the mid-1920s to 1960, includes approximately 1.25 million photographs and is being organized in both subject and biographical categories. Until all the organizing has been completed, the material is available to researchers only by appointment.

The donation of the *World Telegram* clipping files to the University of Missouri School of Journalism has turned out to be a forlorn and distressing matter. Originally contained in 256 three-tiered steel cabinets and 500 storage boxes and housed in an abandoned underground ammunition dump near St. Louis, the files were moved to limestone caves north of Kansas City, and some of these were then transferred to a newly-constructed archival building on the University of Missouri campus in Columbia. The difficulty in making the materials available to researchers and the massive problems related to indexing and retrieval led to the appointment by U. of Missouri President Olson of several history professors to serve on a "World-Telegram Morgue Committee 1982-1983," which decided to have the collection destroyed. Before this action could be taken, however, the University of South Carolina College of Journalism intervened and asked that the collection be given to their institution. Using a grant from the Hearst Foundation, the collection was converted to microfilm and the paper materials were soon thereafter destroyed. Therefore, a paper archive of the *World-Telegram* no longer exists, nor has an article index for it been created. It exists now only in a microform.

According to an August 2002 Associated Press report, however, new technology developed by ProQuest, an Ann Arbor, Michigan, company, may make it possible for researchers to use the Internet to read and to conduct research in these early newspapers. ProQuest has already scanned back issues of both the *Wall Street Journal* from 1889 to 1985 (some one million pages) and the *New York Times* from 1851 to 1999 (some 3.4 million pages). The more recent issues of these newspapers were already available electronically. Both the *Washington Post* and the *Christian Science Monitor* are also being scanned; their archival issues may be made available in 2003. Eventually, according to a ProQuest representative, regional newspapers may in time also be scanned. The most difficult challenge, scanning newspapers in microforms which were themselves filmed from printed texts at various times and with varying results, seems to have been mastered via the development of a special software program which is able both to clean up the scans and to "read" the newspapers in such a way as to make them searchable via Internet websites.

Recently Nicholson Baker has been taking up the cudgels to preserve significant daily newspapers from both the fate of decay and of their preservation solely via microforms. One of his interests is the *World-Telegram*; reading one issue from the February 1934, volume which he had purchased from Timothy Hughes, Baker came across an uncollected Mitchell article reporting on "the arrival of Emma Goldman in the United States after years of exile."

The forthcoming biography of Mr. Mitchell by Thomas Kunkel—because of Mr. Kunkel's access to material in the estate of Joseph Mitchell—will doubtless bring to light more information about his uncollected reportage, such as profiles he did of Eleanor Roosevelt and of the anthropologist Franz Boas.

I have listed here neither Mr. Mitchell's contribution of the story "Cool Swamp and Field Women" to the *New American Caravan* (1929) nor a similar contribution of the story "The Brewers" to the *American Caravan IV* (1931). These narratives (which are evocative of of the Southern agrarian movement of that time and place) are primarily set in swamp land of the South such as he was familiar with in the Ashpole Swamp area south of Fairmont; they are ripe with imagery and atmosphere. They also reveal a willingness, even an eagerness, to use inverted sentence structures, varied sentence lengths, similes, a bit of poetic alliteration, and earthy locutions to create strong sensual impressions and are greatly different from the narratives that would appear a few years later in his first collection, *My Ears Are Bent* (1938). Especially absent here in comparison to his later writing are concreteness of setting, depiction of characters in detail, and realistic dialogue. But the fact alone that his work was appearing along with that of Jean Toomer, Erskine Caldwell, e.e. cummings, Stanley Kunitz, William Carlos Williams, Robert McAlmon, Robert Cantwell, Robert Penn Warren, James Henry Sullivan, John Gould Fletcher, Yvor Winters—and perhaps most notably his mentor and professor Paul Green—became significant in establishing name recognition and an early "track record."

Even earlier than these two contributions, Joseph Mitchell had honed his skills as a reporter for the *Daily Tar Heel*. He often covered the activities of the Carolina Playmakers, which were under the guidance of Paul Green. In Green's classes he had learned a philosophy of literature and a lasting interest and respect for the great Russian writers; Dostoevsky's *The Brothers Karamazov* became a personal favorite. With the advice and advice and encouragement of Green (who won the Pulitzer Prize for *In Abraham's Bosom* while Mitchell was at Chapel Hill), he even tried his hand at writing plays. He contributed, as Paul Maliszewski has discovered, a couple of essays to *The New Student*, a national student magazine that had some similarity to *The New Masses*. A couple of his poems appeared in *Carolina Magazine*. Perhaps most important to his early apprenticeships, however, was a stint with the *Chapel Hill Weekly*, to which he contributed articles connected mostly with university life. He told me, for example, that his knowledge of geology stemmed in large part from a piece he did for the *Chapel Hill Weekly* about a University of North Carolina professor of that subject.

Joseph Mitchell's earliest contribution to a New York newspaper, a study of the Fairmont tobacco market—a version of which had been earlier printed in *Carolina Magazine*—evidently appeared in the Sunday magazine of the *New York Herald Tribune* in the summer of 1929. So far, however, after a couple of lengthy searches in microforms in the New York Public Library, I have been unable to locate this piece. Joseph Mitchell indicated to me in 1995 that it was among his papers.

The *New Yorker* publications listed below do not include any of Joseph Mitchell's unsigned "Talk of the Town" pieces. He said (Interview of 6/19/95) that these were few and of "little consequence." Finally, the records of Joseph Mitchell's publications that are housed in the *New Yorker's* own library and what I have listed below may not be identical; the Library's records are based on the "city edition" of the magazine, and I have relied on microform and print versions of the "national" or "out-of-town" edition.

Finally, I have not listed separately Joseph Mitchell's eulogy of A. J. Liebling, which he read at funeral services held on December 30, 1963; it is reprinted in Raymond Sokolov's *Wayward Reporter*, 321-323; and the second and fourth paragraphs from it are reprinted as part of Section 34 ("A. J. Liebling") of James Barbour and Fred Warner's edition of *Liebling at The New Yorker: Uncollected Essays* (University of New Mexico Press: 1994).

Signed Publications of Joseph Mitchell in The New Yorker

"Profiles"

March 3, 1934. "Home Girl": 25-29. [About *Kate Smith and her "quite tragic two hundred and twenty-six pounds." Smith tells Mitchell, "I'm big and I'm fat and I'm not a prize beauty, but I have a voice, and when I sing, boy, I sing all over."] Never reprinted.

November 4, 1939. "The Marker": 20-27. [*Joe Madden, saloon keeper at 227 West 51st Street and elsewhere, his prose style, and his interest in prizefighting.] Never reprinted.

April 3, 1940. "The Old House at Home": 20-26. [*McSorley's Ale House.] Abridged and reprinted as "Old House at Home" in *Reader's Digest* 37: 71-74, July 1940. Reprinted as first item in *MWS*.

August 3, 1940. "Lady Olga": 20-28. [*Jane Barnell, a bearded lady.] Reprinted in *MWS*. Reprinted by Kevin Kerrane and Ben Yagoda in *The Art of Fact: A Historical Anthology of Literary Journalism* (1997).

September 21, 1940. "Second-Hand Hot Spots": 24-31. [*J. Arthur Granger, who became wealthy during prohibition equipping speakeasies, considers himself more a gambler than a businessman.] Never reprinted.

December 21, 1940. "Mazie": 22-31. [*Mazie Gordon, Bowery philanthropist; earlier newspaper version collected in *My Ears Are Bent*.] Abridged and reprinted in *Reader's Digest* 38: 45-49, March 1941. Also included in Brooks, Purser, and Warren's popular college anthology of literature. Reprinted in *MWS*. The author Fannie Hurst described her friend Mazie, according to William S. Lynch in *Saturday Review of Literature*, as "the most compassionate person I have ever known." An earlier version of this profile, which appeared in the *World-Telegram*, was published in *Ears*.

November 1, 1941. "The Tooth": 24-38. [*Commodore Dutch, his "Association," and his annual ball for the benefit of himself.] Reprinted as "A Sporting Man" in *MWS*.

August 15, 1942. "King of the Gypsies": 21-34. [*Cockeye Johnny Nikanov, urban gypsy lord.] Reprinted in *MWS*. See also "The Beautiful Flower," below.

December 12, 1942. "Professor Sea Gull": 28-43. [*Joseph Ferdinand Gould, Harvard graduate, Greenwich Village street person, and author of "The Oral History of the World."] Reprinted in *MWS* and in *JGS*.

July 24, 1943. "A Spism and a Spasm": 23-37. [Street preacher the *Reverend James Jefferson Davis Hall.] First reprinted in *Up* but under the *MWS* heading.

January 1, 1944. "The Mayor of the Fish Market": 25-34. [Hugh G. Flood, a "composite" or fictional character.] This piece (retitled "Old Mr. Flood") and two "Reporter at Large" pieces following (11/25/44 and 8/4/45) were collected to make up *Flood* (1948).

January 4, 1947. "Dragger Captain I—The Pink Lace Shimmy in the Hell Hole": 32-43. [*Ellery Franklin Thompson, a fish boat captain and a Connecticut Yankee, is a member of a family "that has fished and clammed and crabbed and attended to lobster traps on these waters for over three hundred years."] This piece and the next merged to become the "Dragger Captain" section of *Bottom* (1960).

January 11, 1947. "Dragger Captain II—Professors Aboard": 30-42. [See preceding item.]

January 6, 1951. "The Bottom of the Harbor": 36-52. Drawings by Saul Steinberg. Reprinted as the first section in *Bottom*.

June 28, 1952. "The Cave": 32-55. [*Sloppy Louie Morino's restaurant at 92 South Street.] Reprinted under the title of "Up in the Old Hotel" in *Bottom*.

June 4, 1955. "The Beautiful Flower": 39-80. [Police Captain *Daniel J. Campion and the urban gypsy criminal culture. Along with "King of the Gypsies" it was the basis for the Broadway musical *Bajour*.] Retitled "The Gypsy Women" and added to the *MWS* section of *Up*.

September 22, 1956. "Mr. Hunter's Grave": 50-89. [*George H. Hunter of South Shore, Staten Island. Mitchell believed this piece to be his best work.] Reprinted in *Bottom* and given the honor of first position in David Remnick's collection of *NY* profiles in his 2000 book, *Life Stories: Profiles from The New Yorker*. (See also the entry on Mary Hawthorne, following.)

April 4, 1959. "The Rivermen": 42-111. [*Edgewater, New Jersey, and *Harry Lyons and friends in retrospective talk.] Reprinted in *Bottom* and in Sims's and Kramer's *Literary Journalism*.

September 19, 1964. "Joe Gould's Secret—I": 61-125. [The first installment of Mitchell's second profile of *Joseph Ferdinand Gould, his most full-bodied, perplexing, and troublesome character.] Reprinted as first part of the second section of *JGS*.

September 26, 1964. "Joe Gould's Secret—II": 53-151. [Second installment and Joseph Mitchell's last signed piece in *NY*.]

"A Reporter at Large"

November 11, 1933. "They Got Married in Elkton": 36-43. [Story of the *Reverends Moon and Minor and the marriage industry in *Elkton,

Maryland.] Never reprinted. (Joseph Mitchell, were he still alive, would have enjoyed reading the article on Elkton in the February 2002 *National Geographic*, which features the Zip Code for Elkton, 21921, under the series title "Zip USA." Having been inspired by a 1913 Delaware law which mandated a four-day waiting period for prospective couples, this enterprise has survived seventy years since Mitchell first wrote about it, lasting longer than most of the recurring events and institutions—and certainly of any of the people—about whom he wrote. Well-known celebrities who have been married in Elkton include Billie Holiday, Willie Mays, Jersey Joe Walcutt, Charles Barkley, Ethel Merman, Bert Lahr, Joan Fontaine, John Eisenhower, and Pat Robertson. Mitchell's fascination with the marriage industry may have been sparked by a similar enterprise in Dillon, South Carolina, not but about twenty or so miles from his native Fairmont, North Carolina.)

November 21, 1936. "Bar and Grill": 66-71. [Profile of *Dick's Bar and Grill; its eccentric denizens and the gaming and gamesmanship going on there; it and a later treatment ["Obituary of a Gin Mill"—see later] of this venue after Dick gentrifies it in a new location anticipate Mitchell's later, greater profile of *McSorley's Old Ale House.] This version of Dick's was reprinted in *Ears*.

July 3, 1937. "Mr. Grover A. Whalen and the Midway": 22-26. [Profile of dancers at the New York World's Fair, in particular *Florence Cubitt, "Queen of the Nudists at the California Pacific International Exposition at San Diego in 1936."] Never reprinted.

August 27, 1938. "Hit on the Head with a Cow": 21-24. [Study of *"Captain Charlie's Private Museum for Intelligent People."] Reprinted in *MWS*.

December 24, 1938. "The Cave Dwellers": 22ff. [In the winter of 1933 Mitchell had pursued the story of a man and woman who had lived in a cave in Central Park for almost a year until a benefactor had put them up in a furnished room in a brownstone near the park. Mitchell's story—apparently in the *World-Telegram*—resulted in a number of offers of money and a job and ultimately in *Mr. and Mrs. Hollinan's angry outburst at him for a factual error in the article.] Reprinted in *MWS* and used by Marie Winn, a friend of Mitchell's in his later years, as the context for an esssay in the *Wall Street Journal* about bird watchers. The story's ironic effect is heightened by the reporter's (Mitchell's) assignment to write a "good cheer" type of story for the Christmas season—but the good cheer for his attempts at a charitable gesture turns out to be a "give him hell!" cry from Mrs. Hollinan to her husband, with a bottle of gin being flung after Mitchell as he makes his escape.

January 7, 1939. "Obituary of a Gin Mill": 30-37. [Retrospective on the now-closed former *Dick's Bar and Grill and how "lonesome" Mitchell feels when he walks by the old red-brick building.] Reprinted in *MWS*. An earlier treatment of this establishment appeared in *NY* in 1936 (see above) and was collected in *Ears* as "Bar and Grill" in the "Drunks" section.

February 11, 1939. "The Little Brutes": 37-40. [Profiles of *Rosita Royce, the bubble dancer, and a *dove dancer.] Never reprinted.

April 15, 1939. "All You Can Hold for Five Bucks": 35-42. [A loving study of the *New York Beefsteak Dinner.] Reprinted in *MWS*.

April 29, 1939. "The Catholic Street": 68-74. [A profile of *Barclay Street, its history, its businesses, its church.] Apparently reprinted in *Church Goods Journal* on authority of *NY* archives in New York Public Library.

May 6, 1939. "Houdini's Picnic": 45-55. [*Calypso music in New York City.] Reprinted in *MWS*.

July 29, 1939. "A Mess of Clams": 28-36. [South Bay trip with *Captain Archie M. Clock on the *Jennie Tucker*.] Reprinted under the same title in *MWS*.

October 28, 1939. "Mr. Barbee's Terrapin": 46-51. [Mr. Mitchell moves away from his usual venues to a terrapin farm on the *Isle of Hope near Savannah.] Reprinted under the title "The Same as Monkey Glands" in *MWS*.

March 30, 1940. "Santa Claus Smith of Riga, Latvia, Europe": 39-45. [Profile of *John S. Smith, now perhaps seventy, vagabond and hitchhiker, who writes bogus checks in gratitude for favors as he travels from Louisiana to California and back again about twice a year.] First reprinted, as "Santa Claus Smith," in the *MWS* section of *Up*.

August 31, 1940. "Evening with a Gifted Child": 28-32. [Profile of *Philippa Duke Schuyler, offspring of a black father and white mother and who has a certified I.Q. of 185.] Reprinted in *MWS*. *Reader's Digest* also given permission to abridge and reprint by telegram dated November 6, 1940 (according to archives of *NY* in the New York Public Library). See also entry later under "Talalay" in "Ancillary and Corollary Sources."

May 3, 1941. "Mr. Colborne's Profanity-Exterminators": 39-54. [Profile of *Arthur S. Colborne, a beer-drinking reformer and President of the Anti-Profanity League.] Reprinted in *MWS* as "The Don't Swear Man." A June 2, 1996, editorial tribute to Joseph Mitchell by Philip Terzian in the *Providence Sunday Journal* also used the title "The don't swear man."

September 20, 1941. "But There is No Sound": 54-66. [Profile of the *Union League of the Deaf, *Samuel Frankenheim, and *Jack Fitzsimmons.] Reprinted under the title of "The Deaf-Mutes Club" in the *MWS* section of *Up*.

April 29, 1944. "Thirty-two Rats from Casablanca": 28-43. [Mitchell's now-classic study of the hidden life of *rats in New York: their family lives and attempts to control their population.] Reprinted in *Bottom* as "The Rats on the Waterfront" and subsequently reprinted in *Writing Creative Nonfiction: The Literature of Reality*, ed. Gay Talese and Barbara Lounsberry. HarperCollins, 1995.

November 25, 1944. "Coffins! Undertakers! Hearses!": 30-45. [Continues the history of the fictional Hugh Griffin Flood begun as a "Profile" in the January 1, 1944, issue.] Reprinted in *Flood*.

August 4, 1945. "Mr. Flood's Party": 22-35. [Concludes the story of Hugh G. Flood, with an apparently unintended allusion to the E. A. Robinson poem.] Reprinted in *Flood*.

September 17, 1949. "The Mohawks in High Steel": 38-53. [A study of the success in the building of high-rise structures by mixed-blood *Caughanawa Mohawks from near Montreal and now in Brooklyn.] Reprinted by Edmund Wilson in *Apologies* (1960) and then added by Mitchell himself to the *MWS* section of *Up*. Joseph Mitchell's interest in the Caughnawaga culture derived in large part from his upbringing in triracial Robeson County, North Carolina, an area in which in fact the Lumbee Indians make up the plurality of citizens. He had immense respect for and interest in the welfare of these people and similarly interest in and respect for what is now the University of North Carolina at Pembroke, which was for most of its history (from 1887 to 1953) restricted solely to the education of the Indians of Robeson County. Throughout his adult life Joseph Mitchell was a subscriber to the *Robesonian*, a newspaper published in Lumberton, the county seat of Robeson County, that he considered as valuable to him as the *New York Times*. Harold Ross was especially pleased with the outcome of this project, telling Mitchell in a memo dated July 26, 1949:

> I would report that I've read the story on the Indians, and that I consider it wonderful. Not only am I gratified at being a party to the publication of such a distinguished piece of writing, but, personally, it takes a great load off my mind: I've been nagged about those Indians in Brooklyn for ten years, and have been lobbying for a story on them most of that time. I never expected one as brilliant as this, but you cast your bread upon the waters and sometimes a miracle occurs.

A summer 2002 exhibit (through October 15) at the National Museum of the American Indian, was titled "Booming Out: Mohawk Iron Workers Build New York." The show was conceived in part as a result of the destruction of the twin towers of the World Trade Center on September 11, 2001 (the museum is near "Ground Zero"). The show chronicles the contributions made by the Akwesane and Kahnwake (or "Caughnawaga") nations of the Mohawks over six generations and more than a hundred years to the building of the bridges and skyscrapers of New York City.

Fiction

June 4, 1938. "The Kind Old Blonde": 26. ["Fly-on-the-wall" story about Jim and his big, brassy blonde, who convinces him to drink in spite of a doctor's orders.] First reprinted in the *MWS* section of *Up*.

November 5, 1938. "Mrs. Bright and Shining Star Chibby": 19-21. [His wife having been converted by Father Divine, Mr. Chibby, a black barber and sometime mate on a party boat out of Sheepshead Bay, explains to the narrator how he got his bandaged head.] Never reprinted; a somewhat similar theme is developed in "I Blame It All on Mamma."

December 10, 1938. "I Couldn't Dope It Out": 78-80. [Says the narrator, he returned to My Blue Heaven Café and Restaurant in Hoboken after disembarking from a Hog Island freighter just returned from Copenhagen. There is a debate about the upcoming fight between Joe Louis and "Two-Ton" Tony Galento.] First reprinted in the *MWS* section of *Up*.

January 14, 1939. "The Downfall of Fascism in Black Ankle County": 16-21. [One of his three stories set in Black Ankle County (his equivalent for Robeson County), North Carolina, this is the "closest to home" of Mitchell's early pieces in *NY*.] Reprinted in *MWS*, in E. B. and Katharine White's *A Subtreasury of American Humor* (1941), and in *Fifty Great American Short Stories*, Ed. Milton Crane (Bantam Books, 1965 et seq.). This humorous account of the collapse of the Ku Klux Klan was in part based on events in and around Fairmont ("Stonewall" here). In talking with young Joseph about a relative of theirs who had Klan sympathies, his father, A. N. Mitchell, told him, "Son, you don't take the law into your own hands." Joseph Mitchell also told me in June of 1995, "My father was old-fashioned in many ways, but as far as race was concerned, he made no differences, as long as you worked." There was one black farmer, in fact, that A. N. would buy land for, conveying it to him for what he had paid for it: at a time when a black man could not purchase land on his own in Robeson County. And A. N.'s integrity was perhaps the primary reason why his tenants stayed loyal to him: they trusted him. (For more information about A. N. Mitchell, see the entry on *Flood*).

May 13, 1939. "Uncle Dockery and the Independent Bull": 41-43. [Another story set in Stonewall in Black Ankle County, this one about the cantankerous Uncle Dockery Fitzsimmons and his most famous escapade.] Reprinted in *MWS*. In the Winter 2000 issue of *Southern Culture* (in which Mitchell is pictured on the cover and again in the interior in the photograph by Anne Hall which was used on the back cover of *Up*), "The Dead Mule Rides Again," a well-researched and well-written article about the mule in Southern life and literature, makes reference to this story, noting how Uncle Dockery, in disgust and disdain with the hand that Fate had dealt him by killing off his two mules (they "got sick and died of…vesicular stomatitis or horsepox"), hooked himself up to his bull in order to haul home some firewood in a wagon. The results are predictable: traumatic for Uncle Dockery, and amusing to the reader.

May 27, 1939. "The Hospital Was All Right": 59-60. [Set on a Fifth Avenue bus, a "slice-of-life" narrative of a girl just released from Bellevue with her new baby—and her conversation with her boyfriend, the putative father.] Never reprinted.

September 16, 1939. "Goodbye, Shirley Temple": 17-18. [Set in Madame Visaggi's restaurant, this narrative is concerned with a familiar customer's birthmark, a young girl's curiosity about it, and dice games.] First reprinted in *Short Stories from the New Yorker*. Reprinted in *MWS*.

December 2, 1939. "Saturday Night Was a Dangerous Night": 29-31. [Mike falls off the wagon after six weeks of lonely abstinence.] Reprinted as "On the Wagon" in *MWS*.

January 13, 1940. "I Blame It All on Mamma": 19-22. [Story of Mrs. Copenhagen Calhoun, cook, drunk, dysfunctional wife, who ends up throwing the "Running Riverites" Baptists into the river in order to save her marriage.] Reprinted in *MWS* and subsequently in *Roy Blount's Book of Southern Humor*, ed. Roy Blount, Jr. W. W. Norton, 1994.

Books and Contributions to Books in Chronological Order

My Ears Are Bent. New York: Sheridan House, 1938. A collection composed almost entirely of Mr. Mitchell's newspaper pieces from the *New York Herald Tribune* and the *New York World-Telegram*. His introduction to this extremely rare book, also titled "My Ears Are Bent," is of particular interest, as is his account of coverage of the Lindbergh trial, his interview with the aging evangelist Billy Sunday, and his reportage of events and people in Harlem, most significantly in his account of the voodoo trade in New York City. A good many of his subjects and themes prefigure the later, more reflective studies of Manhattan "pilgrims" in *NY*. The dust jacket is whimsically illustrated with photos of the author taken by Therese Mitchell in their Greenwich Village apartment. The only one of Mr. Mitchell's books without a dedication. However, the handsome new Pantheon Edition of June, 2001 (edited by Dan Frank) has been newly dedicated to Mitchell's last surviving sibling, (William) Harry Mitchell, and his wife Florence. Under the title of "Showmanship," newspaper articles about George Bernard Shaw, Gene Krupa, and George M. Cohan are also collected. Four pieces are subtracted from the "It's a Living" section, and four new pieces are added. The entirety of Section VIII ("Our Leaders") has been deleted in favor of "Showmanship," no doubt because both Frank and Sheila McGrath recognized the ephemerality of this material. Mitchell's interviews and stories about other celebrities of his day, such as *Eleanor Roosevelt, the anthropologist *Franz Boas, *Albert Einstein, *Bing Crosby, *Frida Kahlo, *Clara Bow, *Emma Goldman, *Rudy Vallee, *Joe Louis, *Noël Coward, *Tallulah Bankhead, *Helen Morgan, and *Fats Waller have not yet been collected or reprinted. A number of prominent reviewers in 1992 of *Up in the Old Hotel* (e.g., Roy Blount Jr., Mindy Aloff) seem to have been entirely unaware of the existence of Mitchell's 1938 collection.

McSorley's Wonderful Saloon. New York: Duell, Sloan, and Pearce, 1943. A "War Edition. This book is produced with the conservation orders of the War Production Board." A collection of Mr. Mitchell's early *NY* pieces; a couple of the pieces first appeared in other versions in the *New York World-Telegram*. This book has been his most popular one; it had gone through nine printings by the time *Bottom* was published in 1960. Perhaps the primary reason for its enduring popularity is that it provides the reader, as Lewis Gannett pointed out in an early review in the *Herald Tribune*, the opportunity to "renew his faith in the possibilities of human nature," badly needed as a tonic in the middle of the Second World War and in the encroachments upon vulnerable humanity—then and later—by the yammering demons of technology. In 1944 "Blue Ribbon Books" brought out an almost-identical version to the original (including dust jacket) but reduced in size from 8 5/16" x 5 3/4" to 7 7/16" x 5 ½". Notwithstanding Mitchell's later animadversions against having his books reprinted in paperback, there are also four North American paperback editions of *MWS*. In Canada a "Collins White Circle Pocket Novel" (#208) was published in 1944. A Penguin New York edition (#557) appeared in 1945 and also a Grosset & Dunlap Universal Library edition (UL-60), putatively in 1943. Booksellers also may list a "July 1953" Harlequin Mass Market paperback. *MWS* brought Mitchell international attention from such British reviewers as A. A. Milne, Peter Quennell, and John Betjeman, and a significant early review in the *New Republic* by Malcolm Cowley. Included here are five pieces which Mitchell, in the "Author's Note" to *Up*, would openly avow as fictional. The fifteen nonfiction items are uniformly excellent, but the pieces originally published in *NY* as "Profiles," particularly those of *Mazie Gordon, *McSorley's, *Commodore Dutch, *Cockeye Johnny Nikanov, *Jane Barnell, and *Joe Gould, have gotten the most attention. Mitchell later was to add several items to the *MWS* section of the 1992 anthology: see following. Dedicated to Mr. Mitchell's wife, Therese. Pantheon, with editor Dan Frank and "Foreword" by Calvin Trillin, reissued in June 2001 the *MWS* material that had appeared in *Up* under this title; they included a portrait by Anne Hall of the author in a library setting on the reverse of the dust jacket. In conjunction with the release of the 2001 edition, Mr. Trillin and Eli Wallach (who had done a series of readings from Mitchell's work on BBC radio in 1993) conducted a "sold out" public reading from "The Old House at Home" at McSorley's Old Ale House. The director of publicity for Pantheon, Sophie Cottrell, said of this event: "It was wall-to-wall Joe Mitchell fans and it was great. The back room was so packed, you could not move. The crowd was spilling out into the main part of the bar and it was a really nice evening." (qtd. in McEvoy, p. 79). A number of artists have used *McSorley's Old Ale House as the setting for some of their most recognizable paintings or drawings. The most prominent of these was John Sloan (1871-1951) whose first painting (of five) dates to 1912. Sloan, usually but perhaps too neatly linked with those known as the "Ashcan School," might be pleased to find his McSorley's paintings placed in such diverse locales as the Detroit Institute of Arts, the University of Nebraska, the Delaware Art Museum, Dartmouth College, the Joseph Hirshorn Foundation of New York City, and the John Sloan Trust.

Old Mr. Flood. New York: Duell, Sloan, and Pearce, 1948. A sequence of one "Profile" ("The Mayor of the Fish Market," January 1, 1944) and two "Reporter at Large" articles ("Coffins! Undertakers! Hearses!" on November 25, 1944; and "Mr. Flood's Party" on August 4, 1945) from *NY*. In his introduction Mitchell offers the disclaimer that Mr. Flood was a composite character and that he wanted "these stories to be truthful rather than factual, but they are solidly based on facts." For whatever reason, although Mr. Mitchell notes that it "sold pretty well," *Flood* was sparsely reviewed; in our conversation in his office on June 19, 1995, Mr. Mitchell told me that such relatively slight attention may have been caused by its being a small book; and he said that book reviewing, like the writing of obituaries, is somewhat of an accidental business. Another factor may have been that he was venturing into what Tom Wolfe, twenty-five years later, would address as the "New Journalism"; Wolfe therefore gave cachet to what Mitchell (and A. J. Liebling) had already firmly established. Dedicated by the author to his father, A. N. Mitchell. The eponymous main character's given names derive from those of Joseph Mitchell's paternal great-grandfather, Hugh Griffin Mitchell, who died December 10, 1908, a few months after Joseph Mitchell's birth. It is somewhat ironic to realize that while Joseph Mitchell in 1992 openly admitted that *Flood* was fictional, this book is also the closest in tone and spirit to the truths and facts of his own upbringing. The temperament and philosophy of Hugh Flood closely parallel those of his father: both are skilled, experienced businessmen and while often taciturn are also willing to speak out when speaking out demands to be done. Joseph Mitchell told me in 1995 that two facsimiles for his father that he found in New York were "Mr. Ross" and George H. Hunter—see the entry on "Mr. Hunter's Grave." In an essential 1992 essay, Christopher Carduff observed that Joseph Mitchell gave much of himself to Mr. Flood: his "gustatory predilections," his love of the Bible, Mark Twain, Heywood Broun, all things old. Even more compelling may be the fact that he also gave Mr. Flood his own birthday: July 17.

"The Mohawks in High Steel." The introductory chapter to Edmund Wilson's *Apologies to the Iroquois.* New York: Farrar, Strauss, and Cudahy, 1959; Farrar, Strauss, and Giroux, 1960; also a Vintage Book. *Apologies* was reprinted by Octagon Books in 1978 and by Syracuse University Press in 1992, the latter book with a new introduction by William N. Fenton. It has also been translated into several languages. "Mohawks in High Steel," an account of the riveting gangs of the *Caughnawaga Indians of Canada and their colony in the North Gowanus area of Brooklyn, was originally published as what turned out to be Mitchell's last "Reporter at Large" piece in *NY* (September 17, 1949). Here Mitchell's writing gains both energy and significance from his knowledge and appreciation of the Lumbee Indians of his native Robeson County. Wilson's contributions, somewhat revised, also originally appeared in *NY.* "The Mohawks in High Steel" was reprinted in the *MWS* section of *Up* and subsequently in the 2001 Pantheon edition of *MWS.*

The Bottom of the Harbor. Boston: Little, Brown, [1960]. Drawings by Saul Steinberg. The British Chatto and Windus edition appeared in 1961. Some booksellers may give the date of the first American edition as 1959.

A collection of six pieces from *NY* contributions of Joseph Mitchell from April 19, 1944 ("Thirty-two Rats from Casablanca," retitled "The Rats on the Waterfront") to April 4, 1959 ("The Rivermen"), all set in, around, and under New York Harbor. Here Mitchell begins to weave the additional fabric of symbolic, quasi-allegoric structures by means of his three-dimensional—or round—characters (even the rats) and his dynamically vital, sensuously complex settings with a latent threnody of the still, sad music of humanity. "The Rivermen" is included in Norman Sims's and Mark Kramer's *Literary Journalism* (1995), "The Rats on the Waterfront" in *Writing Creative Nonfiction* (1995), and "Mr. Hunter's Grave" in *Life Stories: Profiles from The New Yorker (2000)*. Joseph Mitchell no doubt was particularly pleased to read this sentence from the *Newsweek* article about his work: "His account of an old seaman's hotel, rats and plague, dragger captains and shad fishermen are what James Joyce might have written had he gone into journalism." (A comprehensive comparison of Joyce's fiction and Mitchell's nonfiction narratives must still be made.) Modern Library reissued the entire book in 1994, followed by the British Jonathan Cape reissue in 2000, a reprint of Modern Library's volume in 2000, and a Vintage paperback edition in 2001. The New York Limited Edition Club printed 250 signed and numbered copies of *Bottom* in 1991, with five photogravures by Berenice Abbott—see "Corollary and Ancillary Sources" for information on this photographer. Copies of these books sell on the secondary market for $1000 and up. Dedicated to the author's daughters, Nora and Elizabeth.

Joe Gould's Secret. New York: Viking, 1965. Here Mitchell has brought together in one place the early "Profile" of a "lost soul," *Joseph Ferdinand Gould, from *MWS* (1943: "Professor Sea Gull") and the two-part series titled "Joe Gould's Secret," which was published seven years after Gould's death—as his last contributions—in the September 19 and September 26, 1964, issues of *NY*. The complex, troubling, parasitic, and perhaps ultimately cathartic relationship between subject and author in this book is one of the great enigmas of contemporary letters. Norman Sims has observed, "*JGS* was about Mitchell in the same way that *Ulysses* is about James Joyce." The book and its author's personal involvement in it inspired a provocative film adaption in 2000, directed by and starring Stanley Tucci as Mitchell and Ian Holm as Joe Gould and with the screenplay by Howard Rodman. Mitchell's book was reissued in a Modern Library edition in 1996. A posthumous Modern Library "Commemorative Edition" with an introduction by William Maxwell was issued in October 1996. More recent American editions include a Vintage Paperback edition of

December 1999, with a photo of Joe Gould in Greenwich Village habitat on the dust jacket cover, and a Modern Library reissue with Stanley Tucci (as Mitchell) and Ian Holm (as Gould) pictured on the dust jacket cover. The Jonathan Cape version of the 1996 Modern Library text was published in 1997. There are French, Italian, and German translations. The book was dedicated to the author's three sisters: Elizabeth Mitchell Woodward, Linda Mitchell Lamm, and Laura Mitchell Braswell (now all deceased).

Up in the Old Hotel. New York: Pantheon, 1992. A Vintage soft-cover edition remains in print, still selling thousands of copies a year. A well-crafted and impressively presented anthology gathering all of Mitchell's previous books (except for *Ears*). Edited by Dan Frank (whom Mitchell had first gotten to know when Frank was with Viking) with the assistance of Sheila McGrath. In negotiations with Frank, Joseph Mitchell had indicated that he did not want paperback versions of his work but would consent to a hardbound collection. When Frank replied that such a collection would comprise something over 700 pages, Mitchell, realizing that Frank had already done the layout for the compendium, was taken aback. The only significantly augmented material included in this collection is the approximately 2,000 words which have been added to "The Old House at Home" in the *MWS* section; most of it is connected to the relationship of Mrs. Dorothy O'Connell Kirwin to the business and to her husband's role as manager. (Mrs. Kirwin had inherited the business in 1939 after her father's death.) Mr. Mitchell's "Author's Note" is his first acknowledged published writing since 1965's *JGS*. In it he notes the inclusion of seven pieces to the *MWS* section,* only one of which ("The Mohawks in High Steel" in Edmund Wilson's *Apologies* in 1960), had been previously published. Two of the new items—"The Kind Old Blonde" and "I Couldn't Dope It Out"—are classified as fiction along with the five last pieces from the 1943 edition of *MWS*. Also the "Professor Sea Gull" profile of Joe Gould has been returned to its original place as part of *MWS*. Mr. Mitchell openly admits now that the "three stories in the Flood book are fictional" and that both *Bottom* and *JGS* are factual. Selected by the *New York Times Book Review* as one of the "Notable Books" of 1992 and by *Time* as the second most significant nonfiction book of that year, this anthology also won for Joseph Mitchell the Brendan Gill Award of the New York Municipal Art Society and the Ambassador Book Award for "American Arts and Letters," both in 1993. Widely reviewed across the United States and in England, *Up* was the first book Mitchell—who at his death held all of the copyrights to his books—had, since *MWS*, allowed to be reprinted in paperback. It became one of the Quality Paperback Book Club's most popular choices. Dedicated in its early galleys to "the memory of Averette Nance Mitchell (1881-1976) and Elizabeth Amanda Parker Mitchell (1886-1963) and to the Memory of Therese Dagney Jacobsen Mitchell (1910-1980)," *Up in the Old Hotel* was in its final form dedicated to Sheila McGrath, the author's companion and literary assistant from 1981 until his death in 1996. Ms. McGrath, he believed, had restored his health and perhaps saved his life when he was suffering from a severe case of salmonellosis. In Mr. Mitchell's will she was made an equal heir, along with Nora and Elizabeth Mitchell, to his considerable acreage in Robeson County. Through her literary agent, Henry Dunow, she serves as the formidable executrix of Joseph Mitchell's literary estate.

A Man Named Me. 200?. The purported title—as told by him in 1992 to Margaret Carlin of the *Rocky Mountain News*—of Joseph Mitchell's autobiography and, as he told me at one point or two, the major thrust of his creative endeavors in the last ten or so years of his life. By 1995 he was already negotiating a contract with Pantheon. He told Norman Sims in a 1989 interview that his work on a new book had been slowed considerably by the deaths of his mother (in 1963) and his father (in 1976) and then by civic service in New York from 1982 to 1987: "But despite all these interruptions, down South and up here, I have continued working on a book, and one of these days if I am not terminally interrupted, I hope to finish it." Typically, as he continued to work steadily at his writing in his office at *NY*, he would say little about what he was working on—nor, as consistent with the culture among the writers at the magazine, would his peers or editors dare to inquire about these endeavors. One of his younger and most perceptive friends, Alec Wilkinson (who learned from a messenger that at one time in his office Mitchell had spread out a "huge manuscript"), did learn enough about the memoir he was writing to understand, as he explained in a 1992 *Vogue* essay, that it involved three major parts: one "about his growing up on a tobacco farm in North Carolina (where he still farms and engages in forestry)," another "about his large family," and the last "about his life in the city." Although in his later years he continued to suggest to some interviewers or colleagues that he was working on a book about the Fulton Fish Market, that enterprise essentially ended with the publication of the fictional *Old Mr. Flood* in 1948. (When Tina Brown suggested to him that a disastrous fire at the fish market might provide him a motive to write about its history and importance, he declined to do so.) Also he expressed interest late in life in writing a book about Ann ("Honey") Honeycutt, a glamorous "blonde about town" and the quondam mistress of James Thurber (today a tabloid would write that she was his "arm candy"), but such an endeavor would seem unlikely to keep his creative juices flowing for very long.

*Mr. Mitchell also revised a passage at the end of "A Spism and a Spasm," his July 24, 1943, *NY* profile of a garrulous and poetic street preacher, the Reverend James Jefferson Davis Hall. In the concluding episode (related by the Reverend Hall), Mr. Jones, a derelict alcoholic actor in a fearful and fearsome but funny state of the D.T.'s, falls down the stairs in his dormitory. Nearly two hundred words have been added to the account in *Ears* of this mishap, which provides the author not only the opportunity for Hall to tell the narrator—and the narrator's reader—about his bawdy Alabama grandmother, but also for Mitchell to change the decorous verb "teakettled" to the original, more earthy "ass over teakettle." While we recognize that more authenticity has been restored to this particular passage, we will also better understand why several of Mitchell's "lowlife" articles (on the topic of burlesque queens, for example) have never been collected or reprinted and perhaps also why he was reluctant to assent to a reissue of *Ears* during his lifetime. In addition to a compunction in his mature writings against using some of the vulgar language found in a very few of his original writings (in "My Ears Are Bent," he professed admiration for the "imagery in vulgar conversation"), he seemed also to have felt that his depiction of eccentrics and ethnic minorities in that early collection (especially Jews and "African-Americans") might to some seem patronizing or less than "politically correct." That he was the heir to the endemic culture of his place and time can be seen in his casual use of "nigger" twice in the exposition of his 1929 story, "Cool Swamp and Field Woman," collected in *The New American Caravan*. That the compilers/editors of this collection—Alfred Kreymborg, Lewis Mumford, and Paul Rosenfeld—did apparently not blink at this usage by Mitchell suggests equally as much about this place and time.

Biographies and Biographical Sketches

Kunkel, Thomas. Biography of Joseph Mitchell. Forthcoming from Random House/Pantheon, 2003/2004. Kunkel, Dean of the School of Journalism at University of Maryland since 2000, is also the CEO of the *American Journalism Review,* to which he contributes a monthly column. His 1995 biography of Harold Ross, *Genius in Disguise,* was nominated for a Pulitzer Prize. In our June 1995 visit, Mitchell and I agreed that it was well-researched and well-written but at times puzzlingly organized. Kunkel is also the editor of an absorbing collection of editorial comments by Harold Ross (gleaned from the archives in the New York Public Library), *Letters from the Editor: "The New Yorker's" Harold Ross* (Modern Library, 2000). With the full cooperation of Sheila McGrath, the Executrix of Joseph Mitchell's estate, Kunkel's biography promises to explore and expose nooks and crannies of Mitchell's literary journalism previously kept from public view.

Rundus, Raymond J. *Joseph Mitchell: Pilgrim in Manhattan.* Xlibris, 2002. Because of alleged copyright violations brought to the Production Department of Xlibris by the Henry Dunow Agency (the literary agency representing Sheila McGrath and the Estate of Joseph Mitchell), this appreciative, extensive, and comprehensively indexed study of the genesis and development of Joseph Mitchell as a writer was suppressed by the publisher a week after release and remains under "Cease and Desist!" restraint from Random House, Inc.

Interviews

Mitchell, Joseph. Interview on the "New York and Company" program of WNYC AM on August 28, 1992. With Leonard Lopate. An extensive interview which, by setting out the foundation for his writing career, reveals much about the young Joseph Mitchell.

Mitchell, Joseph. Interview with Mr. Mitchell on "All Things Considered," National Public Radio, August 21, 1992. McSorley's Old Ale House is visited, and passages from Mr. Mitchell's work are read by Tommy Thompson.

Mitchell, Joseph. Personal interview with Mr. Mitchell in his *NY* office at June 19, 1995. Also I have had a number of telephone conversations with Mr. Mitchell—as indicated in the text of this book—and on July 8, 1993, escorted him from his home in Fairmont to a dinner in his honor on the campus of the University of North Carolina at Pembroke.

Perelman, S. J. "S. J. Perelman Takes a Powder." With Peter Taylor. The *Boston Globe* (22 November 1970). Reprinted in *Conversations with S. J. Perelman.* Ed. Tom Teicholz. University Press of Mississippi, 1995.

Singer, Mark. Personal interview with Mr. Singer in his *NY* office June 19, 1995, followed up by a telephone interview on August 28, 1995. Singer, who has been on the staff of *NY* since 1974, is currently charged by David Remnick with writing of the "U.S. Journal" feature, once the domain of Calvin Trillin. His *Mr. Personality* is a collection of profiles, and his profile of the entertainer/illusionist Ricky Jay (also an admirer of Joseph Mitchell) is one of the richest profiles to appear in the magazine in the past twenty years. Singer first became acquainted with the work of Joseph Mitchell in a class with William Zinsser at Yale (with whom he studied the craft of "literary nonfiction" or "creative nonfiction" and with whom he worked for a time on the *Yale University Magazine*), and *Old Mr. Flood* was the first of Mitchell's books that he read. Bill Whitworth, who later served as editor of the *Atlantic Monthly*, became a mentor of Singer's at *NY*. It was Whitworth who advised Singer to familiarize himself with the writing of St. Clair McKelway, Wolcott Gibbs, Russell Maloney, S. N. Berhman, and especially Joseph Mitchell. Singer (later to do an excellent profile of Mitchell in *NY*—see following) first met the older writer on an elevator at the magazine as Mitchell was returning from a funeral. Surprised that this icon at *NY* would know and be interested in *his* work, Singer accepted an invitation to lunch at the Algonquin. Mitchell talked a great deal about James Joyce that day (his beloved "JJ"), and Singer described himself as "amazed that a nonfiction writer would have this kind of interest and such an extensive knowledge."

Trillin, Calvin. "An Interview with Calvin Trillin: 'I'll Just Go and Fix It.'" with John Boe. Reprinted in *Writing on the Edge*, 1992.

Trillin, Calvin. Personal interview by telephone on June 30, 1995. Bob MacMillan, who lived in the same apartment building as Joseph and Therese Mitchell, lent Trillin a copy of *My Ears Are Bent*. Later, in a bookstore in either Portland, Oregon, or Seattle, Trillin was astonished to find a copy of *Ears* marked $3.00. When he was asked "Where'd you get that book?" by the clerk, he was taken aback but willing to even given up his shoes for the book. His apprehension was relieved when he found he had taken the book from a half-price table. Eventually he found another copy that he gave to Mark Singer as a present. Trillin dedicated his collection *Killings* to Joseph Mitchell as the "writer who set the standard."; when Mitchell came to his office to chide him on a similar occasion, he ended the conversation by saying to Trillin, "You're not going to take it back, are you?" In the summer of 1992 Trillin and his wife Alice (also a great admirer of Mitchell's writing) hosted a party in their New York apartment for Mitchell on the occasion of the publication of *Up in the Old Hotel* in 1992, at which event "Bud" Trillin, offered, as one colleague observed, a "memorable toast." Trillin related that at one time he had asked Mitchell about the symbolism that Stanley Edgar Hyman had revealed in his writing, and Mitchell had replied, "Maybe I was thinking above." Trillin believes that A. J. Liebling and Mitchell, in their writing on "lowlife" subjects and themes, had changed the subject matter more than the techniques that their nineteenth-century predecessors had used.

Wilkinson, Alec. "*PW* Interviews: Alec Wilkinson." *Publishers Weekly* (February 1, 1993): 67-68. With Amanda Smith.

Wilkinson, Alec. Personal interviews by telephone on June 30, 1995, and August 16, 1995, and communications on several other occasions. There is no contemporary writer who more admires and appreciates the work of Joseph Mitchell than Alec Wilkinson, who has called him "the artist-reporter of our century." That appreciation derives from his understanding that Mitchell can be approached on several levels: as a stylist, as a reporter who became a peer among equals, as a craftsman with great depth in his construction, and as writer who displayed all of this with "simplicity and offhandedness." Like Stanley Edgar Hyman, Wilkinson believes there is "no other example I know of a writer who has combined so many elements and yet was so innovative.... He is the first and best writer at shading and revealing a character's interior life—the unconscious as part of the conscious life." While Tom Wolfe and Norman Mailer are "self-promoters" who create descriptions only of the "outside world," Mitchell, Wilkinson asserts, had introduced the idea that the "world at large" can be handled fully and figuratively and as something "more than the world we can see before us." Wilkinson, who came on staff at *NY* in 1980, first heard of Joseph Mitchell at a dinner party three years earlier, when his mentor and family friend, William Maxwell, had identified him as "the best writer in America." Intrigued by this judgment, Wilkinson sent on a search to find issues of *NY* in which this writer's articles had appeared, being dismayed to discover that he would have to pay $1200 for magazines containing four of the articles and as much as $450 for a single issue. Eventually he did find and purchase *The Bottom of the Harbor* and *Joe Gould's Secret* and, after he joined the staff of the magazine, resorted to a practice common among his co-workers: making copies of Joseph Mitchell's articles from magazines in the library of *NY*. When he first met Joseph Mitchell in the offices of *NY*, it was for him an "immediately exciting experience." Today he regards Mitchell as a "deeply original American writer"—and for a reader not to know him is the same as playing the alto saxophone without knowing Charlie Parker. (For more on Wilkinson, see the entries under "**Ancillary and Corollary Sources**.")

Bibliography of Secondary Sources

Reviews and Criticism of Joseph Mitchell's Work

Aloff, Mindy. "Joseph Mitchell's Secret." *Threepenny Review* (Spring 1993): 17-19. A former "Talk of the Town" contributor recalls her first encounter with Joseph Mitchell, expresses her appreciation for the strong women in his writing, and ponders the death of William Shawn. A uniquely feminist reading of Mitchell's body of work—especially for Aloff's sympathetic interpretations of "The Beautiful Flower" and "The Old House at Home."

Atkinson, Brooks. "The City's Dockside." [Review of *Bottom*]. *New York Times Book Review* (April 24, 1960); 3, 36. A fellow member of the "Deep Six" group to which Joseph Mitchell belonged, Atkinson here takes on a role somewhat beyond his assignment of reviewing plays for the *Times*. His review is particularly insightful in its description and analysis of Mitchell's role as narrator in these six stories: Atkinson sees his function as that of a guide, and Mitchell is "an unselfconscious writer" who does not criticize or evaluate his strong characters, and "he does not patronize them in any way." Atkinson finds *Bottom* to be literature; it is "beautifully written." The author, though he is "the least described" of the characters in the book, has a "talent for self-effacement [that] is creative. It represents enthusiasm that is muted in style but eloquent in understanding. It represents purity of perception." Atkinson is also sensitive to understanding the theme in these stories of the threat to primeval marine life by the encroachment of "civilization." He seems to identify Joseph Mitchell as an "ecologist" before that term was even in common use.

Baker, Russell. "Out of Step with the World." *New York Review of Books* (September 20, 2001): 10-14. Reviewing the summer 2001 reprintings by Pantheon of *Ears* and *MWS*, Baker spends additional time scrutinizing the Vintage paperback edition of *Up*. He envisions Joseph Mitchell as replacing F. Scott Fitzgerald as the chronicler of "old New York" within a changing city. Baker also draws, as Malcolm Cowley did, some interesting parallels between the London of Dickens and Mitchell's Gotham, but finds the later writer superior as a journalist because of his ability to keep suppressed his passions and his moral perspective. Baker offers a sympathetic commentary on both Jane Barnell and the public persona of her as

"Lady Olga." And he is rightfully intrigued by Joseph Mitchell's modesty as a writer—though Baker's inferences are accurate only about what had been published in the New York newspapers and in *NY*. Mitchell, Baker believes, was unusual among other writers in his saying "not a word about his family history, his childhood, his educational travails, his youthful loves and hates, his early triumphs and humiliations, how he started writing, why he decided to come to New York, or how a self-effacing youngster from the sticks was able to land a job on the elegant *Herald Tribune*." Ultimately, Baker must be added to that growing list of reviewers and critics fascinated by, yet unable to solve, the mystery of Joseph Mitchell's long, seemingly terminal silence as a writer. His unfamiliarity with the long introductory essay to *Ears* ("My Ears Are Bent") suggests that he— and Pete Hamill and Jimmy Breslin too—had been targeted as desirable reviewers of these new editions of Mitchell's writings not because of their intimate familiarity and innate understanding of Joseph Mitchell's repertoire but because they were durable veterans: all "big names" in the business of journalism.

Barnett, Lincoln. "Nostalgic Portraits of the Lunatic Fringe" [Review of *MWS*]. *New York Time Book Review* (July 25, 1943): 5. Barnett's review is somewhat tarnished by his inability to distinguish the nonfiction "stories" from Mitchell's fictional pieces: he believes, for example, that the author grew up in "Black Ankle" (rather than the real Robeson) County. Barnett is keen, however, in his recognition that "Mr. Mitchell is not only a conscientious legman and interviewer, he is also an adroit and sensitive writer."

Bigelow, Scott. "Discovering Mitchell: A Robesonian at The New Yorker." *The Robesonian*, Lumberton, NC (June 4, 2000): 1c,6c. Mr. Bigelow comments on the public vs. the private man, noting that Joseph Mitchell's only "public" appearance as a writer in Robeson County took place on the UNC-Pembroke campus in 1993.

Blount, Roy Jr. "Joe Mitchell's Secret." *The Atlantic Monthly* (August 1992): 97-99. Blount, who had interviewed Mitchell a couple of years earlier concerning a reissue of one of A. J. Liebling's books, speculates on the author's long silence and discusses how he was able to celebrate the lives of characters (especially Joe Gould) who were living precarious existences.

Blount, Roy Jr., ed. *Roy Blount's Book of Southern Humor*. W. W. Norton, 1994. Blount reprints "I Blame It All on Mama," noting that it is one of several of Mr. Mitchell's "semifictional recollections of life back home."

"Bowery Botanist." [Review of *MWS*] *Time* 42 (August 2, 1943): 98, 100. The first sentence of this review provides its thesis: "Joseph Mitchell is as gloomy as only a humorist can be." The reviewer also suggests that e.e. cummings was the first writer to immortalize McSorley's Old Ale House. And a footnote on p. 98 (keyed to a photo of "Harvard's Gould") observes that Joe Gould has reported that Scribner's was interested in publishing a fragment of the "Oral History": "'Willkie called his book *One World*. Mine will be called *A Million Worlds*. There are as many worlds as there are people, each having his own world.' Asked whether he liked his own world, Joe said, 'I haven't decided yet.'"

Breslin, Jimmy. "Another Round: Two rounds of stories, from newsroom and barroom, by Joseph Mitchell." *New York Times Book Review* (June 3, 2001): 34. In his usual breezy and ingratiating style, Breslin does a take on his experience of examining in McSorley's Old Ale House the galley proofs for the Pantheon editions of *Ears* and *MWS*. Breslin ends his review with an account of his being introduced to Joseph Mitchell in Elaine's a few years past. In between he marvels at how this writer was able to make his "social zone...the nearest interesting person." Among those mentioned by Breslin are Mazie Gordon, Peter Arno, and Cockeye Johnny Nikanov. The one topic that he felt Mitchell had scrupulously avoided was race (Breslin seems unfamiliar with the treatment of that topic in *Flood*).

Carduff, Christopher. "Fish-eating, whiskey, death, & rebirth." *The New Criterion* II, No. 3 (November 1992): 12-22. Unfortunately, Carduff's is not an easily accessible study, but it is an expertly incisive and amply documented review of the origins of Joseph Mitchell themes, a useful explanation of his technique: the best short study in print of this author as a writer.

Carlin, Margaret. "Details, Details: Joe Mitchell alive, well, watching." *Rocky Mountain News* (October 4, 1992): 101,103. Somehow Carlin, who apparently interviewed Mr. Mitchell by telephone, was able to wring from him information and opinions—advice from a city editor, how he took notes, Charles Addams, his current reading, the title of his planned autobiography ("A Man Named Me")—found nowhere else.

Carrington, Tucker. "The Grammar of Hard Facts: Joseph Mitchell's *Up in the Old Hotel*." *Virginia Quarterly Review* 72 (Winter 1996): 47-63. While acknowledging that with the publication of *Up* Mitchell had reestablished himself as among the best living American essayists, Carrington believes that the tone of his trumpet is rather "doleful," for there is (1) no longer much of a market for the plain declarative sentence that he writes, and (2) his characters "have turned from a parade of raffish and charming drunks and scalawags into pathetic, shameful statistics." Carrington finds *JGS* to be an "exhausting read" and "the end result [of the longer pair of profiles] is much less satisfying because it lacks a certain verity." Carrington not only appears to be unacquainted with the sophisticated strategies and thematic diversity found in contemporary literary journalism, he also ignores—when he classifies Joseph Mitchell as an "essayist"—the subtle artistry of his subject's narratives. And his judgments about *JGS* ought to be countered by those of such a committed reader and intuitive judge as Alec Wilkinson, who told me he regarded *JGS* as a "paradigm of organization."

Cohen, Rich. "Joseph Mitchell." *The Oxford American*, Vol. 2 (1992): 50-52. Although Cohen, a true admirer who came during his tenure as a messenger at *NY* to know and deeply respect Joseph Mitchell, risks credibility when he asserts that Joseph Mitchell is from the "rugged hills of North Carolina," his review indicates a common dilemma, that of the enthusiastic reader who has been able, prior to the publication of *Up*, to find Mitchell's writing only in clandestine or bootlegged forms.

Cohen, Rich. *Lake Effect*. Knopf, 2002. Ostensibly a novel, this book (pp. 188-190) recreates a conversation that Cohen, who worked at *NY* at the time, had with Joseph Mitchell in his office a few years before his death. The conversation centers interestingly upon James Thurber's frequent use of the phrase "Too late!" (Thurber also was known for scribbling it along the walls in the office hallways near "Sleepy Hollow.") Both Mitchell and Cohen offer thoughtful reflections upon the significance of the phrase.

Core, George. "Wonderful eccentrics reside at 'Old Hotel.'" *Washington Times* (September 13, 1992): B7. Mr. Core, editor of the *Sewanee Review* and frequent writer about *NY*, regards Dan Frank, Mitchell's editor at Pantheon, as the second hero of the 1992 compilation: Core places Mitchell in first position among journalists, a "reporter for all climes and seasons."

Cowley, Malcolm. "Joseph Mitchell: The Grammar of Facts." In *The Flower and the Leaf: A Contemporary Record of American Writing Since 1941*. Ed. and with an introduction by Donald W. Faulkner. Viking, 1985. Cowley (still widely regarded as the scholar/critic who brought William Faulkner to prominence) writes an essay that is truly "seminal" in foregrounding Joseph Mitchell as a journalist worthy of attention as a significant figure in the history of American letters. This essay was originally published as a review of *MWS* and appeared in the July 26, 1943, *New Republic*.

Denby, David. "The Current Cinema." [Review of Film] *The New Yorker* (April 10, 2000): 100-101. Denby commends Stanley Tucci for creating a "more generous New York, mellow as amber," but he can't get a handle on the real point of the movie in relation to the Mitchell/Gould symbiosis.

Dirda, Michael. *"My Ears Are Bent." Washington Post* (June 10, 2001): BW15. Speaking of the collected work of Joseph Mitchell in 1992's *Up*, Dirda sees now that this compendium was "a touchstone, the best in show, a work of art transcending, or even justifying, its genre. In New York's panhandlers and street evangelists, watermen and con artists, Mitchell discovered both an Old Testament grandeur and a no-nonsense acceptance of the world's fundamental bittersweetness...." He thinks, in fact, that Mitchell fares well in comparison to Mark Twain and James Joyce, Mitchell's two favorite writers. Dirda, who searched for years in bookstores for his own copy of *Ears* and finally resorted to photocopying the entirety of Duke University library's copy, feels—in a deliberate understatement—that "It's good to see this book back in print."

Epstein, Bennett. "All Around the Area with J. Mitchell." [Review of *The Bottom of the Harbor*] *New York Herald Tribune Book Review* (May 8, 1960): 4. Epstein identifies "Mr. Hunter's Grave" (so also Mitchell's favorite piece) as the "gem" of this collection. Perhaps ignoring—as other reviewers also have—"The Rats on the Waterfront," Epstein finds a common theme in Mitchell's stories: "Each of the men pictured here lives in a world of his own which, under Mr. Mitchell's perceptive and appreciative guidance, the reader is allowed to enter for a while and remember with warm pleasure afterward."

Epstein, Joseph. "Joe Gould's Masterpiece." *New Republic* (October 23, 1965): 26-30. A solid if undistinguished summary and commentary on the secret that Joe Gould harbored and cherished in Joseph Mitchell's "wonderful book about it."

Epstein, Joseph. "Talk of the Town: Joseph Mitchell." *The Times Literary Supplement* (September 4, 1992): n.p. The editor of the *American Scholar* reviews the vintage years of the *New Yorker*, marvels at the work that both A. J. Liebling and Joseph Mitchell accomplished under the editorship of William Shawn, and expresses grave concerns about the current state of the journal as Tina Brown (who had made *Vanity Fair* an "editors' magazine") assumed the helm.

Ferguson, Otis. "About People." *New Republic* (March 3, 1938): 108. A review of *My Ears Are Bent.*

Gehman, Richard. "Men about Manhattan." [Reviews together *The Bottom of the Harbor* and Meyer Berger's *Meyer Berger's New York*] *Saturday Review of Literature* 43 (July 9, 1960): 17. Gehman laments two losses here: the death of Berger and the low productivity of Joseph Mitchell. He does find that both worked in different fashion in the same territory and produced a body of work that can be termed "classic." Gehman also observes with some acuteness that "Mitchell is not interested in many different things, but he is interested in everything about the ones that do attract him."

Grimes, William. "A Listener Bends the Ear of Another." *New York Times* (July 22, 1992): C13, C17. A well-informed and insightful retrospective on the career of Mr. Mitchell on the eve of publication of *Up*: part of this interview was conducted in McSorley's Old Ale House.

Hackett, Thomas. "Gentlemanly Writer Comes Home: Robeson County Native Joseph Mitchell is Buried." *The News and Observer* (Raleigh, N.C.), May 29, 1996. The writer has interviewed Mr. Mitchell's surviving brother, Harry; one of his two surviving sisters (Linda Lamm); and Roy Wilder, Jr., a North Carolinian who was a contemporary of Mr. Mitchell's in New York journalism. Also features a 1993 AP photo of Mr. Mitchell in his *NY* office.

Hamill, Pete. "News That Stays News." *Los Angeles Times* (June 17, 2001): n.p. [A review of the 2001 Pantheon editions of *Ears and* MWS]. Like two other world-class journalists of our day, Jimmy Breslin and Russell Baker, Hamill is enamored of the manner in which Joseph Mitchell transcended the usual limitations of his profession: "In his lucid, sturdy prose he achieved what is usually associated only with the finest literary writers: the creation of a personal world." As with several other observers, including in his later years Mitchell himself, Hamill attributes Mitchell's failure to continue writing for publication after the mid-1960s to a sea change in the mores and manners of American culture, in particular the lack of good and colorful and rich talk. Hamill is grateful for these two new books—for we now "have more of Mitchell's books than we have had for decades. His pieces, his vision, his gift of listening have much to teach young writers and editors. But they will be a revelation for younger readers too. They are reports from a lost world, and they are literature too: news that stays news."

Hawthorne, Mary. "Diary." *London Review of Books* (August 1, 1996). Hawthorne, a Briton who worked at *NY* for fifteen years, had not become personally acquainted with Joseph Mitchell until 1995 (the year before his death), when he invited her into his office to discuss Walker Evans, about whom she was researching and writing. She finds that Mitchell admired Evans in his earlier photography for his ability (like that of Diane Arbus) to *see things*. Then, suggesting to Hawthorne a considerable amount of self-revelation, he says,

But then the world changes. You can lose your subject. And you can't *see* things the way you once did. You know, Diane Arbus. Diane Arbus came along and she could *see* things. But Walker Evans, he couldn't see them anymore.... And through it all, you're always comparing yourself to what you did last. There's that, too. You've always got to do yourself one better.... Gosh Almighty,...who can stand it?

Hawthorne reviews at some length Joseph Mitchell's career, particularly praising his early *NY* profiles of Mazie Gordon and Jane Barnell ("Lady Olga"). Another of her favorites is "Mr. Hunter's Grave," and her reading of it leads her, shortly after Mitchell's death, to go out to Staten Island to find Hunter's home and the cemetery where he was to be buried beside his second wife. In a scene reminiscent of Louie Morino's and Mitchell's visit to the upper stories of the Fulton Ferry Hotel, she and her husband find only Mr. Hunter's deteriorated house, behind which are found lying several wet sheets of the hymn "Under His Wings," from which she quotes several lines. She describes the sights and sounds in and around the cemetery, and she and her husband are "dumbfounded" to find no death date on Mr. Hunter's gravestone. [He was 87 when Mitchell's profile was written in 1956.] She asks herself and us, "Was Mr. Hunter down there somewhere? Or had he ended up in some other, completely unknown place.... Mr. Hunter was right, I thought; it didn't make any difference. And yet it did."

Hyman, Stanley Edgar. "The Art of Joseph Mitchell." *The New Leader* (December 6, 1965): 8-10. Reprinted posthumously in *The Critic's Credentials*, ed. Phoebe Pettengill. Atheneum, 1978. The earliest study of Joseph Mitchell as a literary artist whose work (especially here *Bottom* and *JGS*) will transcend its time and place. Hyman contends that Mitchell's work, anchored in the bedrock of artistic integrity, often has universal and archetypal implications: perhaps unconsciously himself, Mitchell plumbs the depths of the subconscious, especially so in *JGS*, "a Jamesian story of life's necessary illusion.... Gould is a masking (and finally an unmasking) for Mitchell himself.... the body of Mitchell's work is precisely that Oral History of Our Time that Gould himself could not write." The most important of Hyman's revelations is the discovery that nonfiction, when written with the artistry of a Joseph Mitchell, is as much enriched by a symbolic and archetypal structure as are the greatest works of fiction or drama.

"In Lardner's Line." *Time* (February 14, 1938): 66. A brief review of *Ears*.

Ivry, Benjamin. "Joseph Mitchell's Secret." *New York* (February 9, 1987): 20. An anticipation of the publication of *Up* and the only piece in the periodical press by or about the author between 1983 and 1992.

Joe Gould's Secret. Film. Directed by Stanley Tucci and adapted from the novel in the screenplay by Howard A. Rodman. An authentic and well-modulated cinematic adaptation of Joseph Mitchell's 1942 and 1964 studies of his most famous and most puzzling "lost soul," with a dramatization of Mitchell himself, his wife, and their two daughters. Released in April 2000 to limited theater viewing and on videotape in September 2000. An especially revealing portrayal of the intimate relationship between Mitchell (Tucci) and Joe Gould (an outstanding performance by Sir Ian Holm) with carefully crafted portrayals of Therese Mitchell (Hope Davis), Vivian Marquis (Patricia Clarkson), Alice Neel (Susan Sarandon), Harold Ross (a dead-on Patrick Tovatt), and Charles Duell (Steve Martin). An exchange of dialogue between Therese and Joseph Mitchell late at night after a call from Joe Gould suggests the symbiosis of the relationship between author/writer and author/subject:
Therese (Hope Davis): "That was your Mr. Gould."
Joseph (Tucci): "He's not mine."
Therese: "Well, you're his. The story doesn't end just because the writer finishes writing."

Jones, Malcolm. "Books: Mitchell Remembered." In a June 2001 *Newsweek* Web Exclusive, General Editor Malcolm Jones (who also wrote in the magazine in 1992 about the publication of *Up*) ponders the reissue by Pantheon of *Ears* and *MWS*. Jones finds that Mitchell's work "seems greater with every rereading"; he compares the newspaper reportage in the first book to the more reflective and leisurely essays written for *NY* in the second: "Even today [*MWS*] remains an arresting book, heartbreaking, hilarious and humane, and when seen in contrast with the first book, a genuine miracle of stylistic development." And, as he ponders his personal acquaintance with Joseph Mitchell, Jones is moved to write, "…he turned out to be one of the most complex people I've ever met, erudite but endlessly curious, melancholy but unfailingly cheerful, and probably the best example I ever saw of what I think of as the good Southerner…."

Jones, Stephen. "Joseph Mitchell's magic: four gems by a master of melancholy always racing the wrecking ball." *Chicago Tribune* (August 30, 1992): Sec. 14, p. 5. Jones decorates Mr. Mitchell with the title "our poet laureate of entropy."

Kaplan, Fred. "Joseph Mitchell's story makes the screen." *The News and Observer* (Raleigh, NC): 10E, rpt. from *The Boston Globe* (April 20, 2000).

More than a review of the adaptation to the screen of *JGS*, Kaplan's article delves into how Stanley Tucci became enamored of Joseph Mitchell; Kaplan also interviewed David Remnick, current editor of *NY*.

Karpen, Lynn. "Stand at the Bar and Just Listen." *New York Times Book Review* (August 16, 1992): 7. Karpen reports that Mitchell has been "writing all along" and that he is working on two different books: one about the Fulton Fish Market, the other a "complicated biography of a woman [doubtless Ann Honeycutt] about town."

Keenan, John. "Down on the South Shore" [Review of the British Cape Edition of *Bottom*, essentially a reprint of the Modern Library Edition]. *Times Literary Supplement* (September 1, 2000): 21. Keenan derives a theme from Harold Ross's observation—a point also made by James Thurber in his study of Ross—that Joseph Mitchell "presented his editor with a 'special problem...excellent quality, low productivity.'" Keenan asserts that the articles that Mitchell published in *NY* in the 1940s and 1950s had established him as "the finest staff writer in the history of the magazine, and one of the greatest journalists America has produced." He also observes that the best story in *Bottom*, "Mr. Hunter's Grave," needed only "the slightest tweak to turn it into a short story of the highest order."

Kirtz, William. "Last of the Bohemians?" [Review of *JGS*] *Christian Science Monitor* (September 28, 1965): 9. A mixed response to the author's last book, which Kirtz finds to be "sensitive and entertaining, if occasionally mannered," Mr. Mitchell's narrative being sometimes slowed by his "intensely personal tack." This last comment is puzzling and on the surface patently fallacious.

Klinkenborg, Verlyn. "This Was New York. It Was." *New York Times Book Review* (August 16, 1992): 7. Klinkenborg is particularly taken by Mitchell's "geographic imagination" and hopes that *Up* will stay in print "forever."

Koenig, Rhoda. "*Up in the Old Hotel* and Other Stories." [Review] *New York* (August 3, 1992): 56. Not many have written a better sentence about this anthology: "Mitchell has a talent for invention, as shown in the fictional New York stories and those of his North Carolina home, but he has a genius for listening, as is continually revealed in these shimmering pages out of a downtown Arabian Nights."

Leopold, David. "An Oral History of Joe Gould." *New York Times* (March 19, 2000): Section 1, p. 3. Leopold's essay is particularly interesting for what it reveals of the relationship between Al Hirschfeld, William Saroyan, and Gould. Leopold also remarks upon Gould's cameo appearance in William

Burroughs' novel *Naked Lunch* and for being the subject of a poem by Philip Levine, "Joe Gould's Pen."

Lynch, William S. "Raw Onions and No Ladies." [Review of *MWS*] *Saturday Review of Literature* 26 (July 31. 1943): 20. Lynch, like *Nation* reviewer Jerome Millquist, compares Joseph Mitchell's studies of human character in *MWS* to those of O. Henry, especially the latter's *Four Million*. Lynch also praises Mitchell for his recognizing the habitués of saloons for what they are: "…men and women fleeing desperately from the loneliness of the big city—men and women sometimes Homeric, sometimes craven, and frequently tormented by what his Professor Sea Gull calls 'the 3 H's— homelessness, hunger, and hangovers.'"

McEvoy, Dermot. "The Mystery of Joseph Mitchell." *Publishers Weekly* (July 16, 2001): p. 78f. Attention must be paid, according to McEvoy, to the release by Pantheon almost simultaneously of *Ears* and *MWS*. For one thing the New York of these stories offers insights into the New York of today. One valuable topic here is McEvoy's conversation with Dan Frank, Joseph Mitchell's editor at Pantheon and the person largely responsible for the compiling and publication of *Up*. Frank tells McEvoy that reading these two books together will allow Mitchell to reveal himself "to be a writer of the first rank."

McGrath, Charles. "Joyce by the Hudson." *New York Times Magazine* (December 29, 1996): 38. A former staffer at *NY* and putative possible editor offers privileged observations about Mitchell's later years at the magazine and his writing endeavors as he sought to bring forth a "Joycean epic of America…."

Max, Daniel. "Profiles from the Margins." [Review of *Up*] *St. Petersburg Times* (August 9, 1992): n.p. Max suggests that *JGS* marked the change in Mitchell from comedy to tragedy, a change that may have brought about his own demise as a writer (for the first time, one of his characters dies), but Mitchell has left us "a true oral history of our time."

Millquist, Jerome. "Mitchell's Wonderful McSorley's." [Review of *MWS*] *Nation* 157 (August 14, 1943); 190. Like William S. Lynch in *Saturday Review*, Millquist sees O. Henry (whom he refers to as "O'Henry") as in many ways Joseph Mitchell's predecessor. In Mitchell's "sympathetic penetration of life" and in his work as a "scrupulous and attentive writer," Millquist finds parallels to such genre painters as John Sloan (who depicted McSorley's), George Luks, Van Ostade, and Jan Steen.

Mysak, Joe. Review of *Up*. *The American Spectator* (February 1993): 62-63. Mysak's observation that for Joseph Mitchell, "the art was in the writing:

the craft was in the listening" is as good a thumbnail evaluation of his achievement as one will likely find.

Owen, Guy. "Joseph Mitchell." In *Southern Writers: A Biographical Dictionary.* Eds. Robert Bain, Joseph M. Flora, and Louis D. Rubin. Louisiana State University Press, 1979. Owen asserts that Mitchell "has continued to deepen each of his later books by the use of poetic symbolism and folk motifs, notably *Old Mr. Flood* and *Joe Gould's Secret.* In his *New Yorker* profiles he has perfected what has been called [Ed. note: by whom?] 'the urban tall-tale pastoral.'"

Parker, Roy, Jr. "Bookmark: Joseph Mitchell." *The Fayetteville Observer-Times* (August 16, 1992): 16E. Parker offers a brief review of the career of this "Manhattan Meistersinger" and recalls how his father bequeathed him his copy of *Ears.*

Perkins, David. "'I Cover the Waterfront" Indeed: Meet Joseph Mitchell." *Kansas City Star* (June 19, 1994): "Arts," p. 16. Perkins responds to the Modern Library publication of *Bottom* while hailing Joseph Mitchell as the pioneer of "New Journalism."

Perrin, Noel. "Joseph Mitchell: Paragon of Reporters." *Sewanee Review* (Summer 1983): 167-184. An essential and illuminating study of the three phases that Perrin discerned in Joseph Mitchell's celebration of "rowdiness" and in his "immoderate relish" in life. Perrin also asserts that a part of Mr. Mitchell's secret is "that whatever he writes about he tends to know better than anybody else in the world." (Oddly enough, the book that treats the subject that Mitchell knew best, Joe Gould, Perrin considers to be a "lesser work.")

Perrin, Noel. "A Kind of Writing for Which No Name Exists." [*Bottom of the Harbor*] Ch. 4 of *A Reader's Delight.* Published for Dartmouth College by UP of New England. 1988. A succinct and sensible study of Mitchell's fourth book, which along with *MWS*, Perrin believes, mark the best work of "a gardener in a graveyard." Perrin has a blind eye and a deaf ear when it comes to an appreciation of *JGS*, but he regards *MWS* and *Bottom* as "masterpieces," and he particularly loves *Bottom*, having, he says, reread it every four or five years for the past twenty-five years. He believes it possible for some lesser talent to have written "The Rats on the Waterfront," but the other five are a kind of writing

> for which there is no name. Each tells a story, and is dramatic; each is wildly funny and so sad you can hardly bear it; each tells its story so much in the words of its characters that it feels like a kind of apotheosis of oral history. Finally, like the Icelandic sagas, each combines a fierce joy in the physicality of

living with a stoical awareness that all things physical end in
death, usually preceded by years of diminishment. One winds
up admiring Mitchell's characters (all real people [Note: true,
it appears, of at least the cast of characters in *Bottom*]), loving
them, all but weeping for them, maybe hoping to live as gal-
lantly.... I do know that Mitchell has the gift of making roses
bloom in the darkest and least expected places.

Posada, José Guadalupe. *Posada's Popular Mexican Prints*. Selected and edited
by Roberto Berdecio and Stanley Applebaum. Dover, 1972. The only easily accessible collection of Posada's prints for the American reader. (See
the "Special Note" in my Introduction for more about Posada and
Mitchell's appreciation of him.)

"Postscript: JOSEPH MITCHELL. Three generations of New Yorker writers
remember the city's incomparable chronicler." *The New Yorker* (June 10,
1996): 78-83. Memorial remembrances and appreciations from the editors and from Brendan Gill, Roger Angell, Nancy Franklin, Mark Singer,
William Maxwell, Calvin Trillin, Lillian Ross, Janet Malcolm, and Philip
Hamburger. Full page photo of the author taken by Maryland Stuart for
the American Academy of Arts and Letters in 1959.

Powell, Dawn. "Baa, baa black sheep."*Book Week* (September 19, 1965): 8.
Pictured is a heavily-bearded, cigarette-smoking Joe Gould. Like Malcolm
Cowley, Powell sees some similarities between Mitchell and Charles
Dickens. Speculating on the nexus between Gould and Mitchell and
somewhat like Norman Sims in 1990, she suggests that if Joe Gould did
not exist, Joseph Mitchell would have had to invent him.

Rogers, James, and Norman Sims. "Joseph Mitchell." In *American Journalists,
1945-1995: DLB 185*. Based on several extensive interviews that Sims conducted with Joseph Mitchell in connection with his studies of contemporary American literary journalism, this study offers an analysis and
evaluation of the body of his work, with valuable insights into how the
reporter-author selected, approached—and sieved out the nectar from—
his eccentrics and lowlifes.

Rundus, Raymond J. "'Imprisoned by the Past': Joseph Mitchell, Poet Laureate
of Entropy." *Pembroke Magazine 26* (1994), 37-47. A retrospective study of
the primary and secondary material related to Mitchell's literary career.

Rundus. Raymond J. "Joseph Mitchell." *Dictionary of Literary Biography
Yearbook: 1996*. Among other literary figures included in DLB's 1996 ret-
rospective are James Dickey, Ernest Hemingway, Kingsley Amis, and
Orville Prescott, with features on the centenaries of F. Scott Fitzgerald, Ira

Gershwin, and John Dos Passos. A study of both the essential formative influences and considerable literary achievements of the author.

Sachs, Adam. "Joe Mitchell's New York." Photographs by Larry Fink. *GQ* (January 2000): 128-133. Anticipating the soon-to-be-released movie, Sachs and Fink use Greenwich Village streets and the Minetta Tavern ("Gould's unofficial headquarters") as background to Stanley Tucci's poses in his role in the film as Joseph Mitchell, Brooks Brothers suits and all.

Sante, Luc. "Heard on the Street." *New Republic* (October 5, 1992): 43-46. An appreciative, well-balanced assessment of the "unreservedly generous" Joseph Mitchell and what his legacy is to such avid readers as Mr. Sante: now that they can find his works collected under one cover.

Schudel, Matt. "Mitchell's Memory Bank." In the "Book World" column of the *News and Observer* (Raleigh, N.C., August 16, 1992): n.p. A somewhat superficial view of Mr. Mitchell's work, in which Schudel complains about a distressing overuse of quotations (typical, he says, of *NY* writers; one of Mitchell's that he cites as 10 ½ pages long is doubtless the brilliant reverie passage in *JGS*), and he complains that the author once uses "hung" for "hanged"—and implies that he should have been hanged for not knowing better.

Severo, Richard. "Joseph Mitchell, Chronicler of the Unsung and the Unconventional, Dies at 87." *The New York Times.* National Edition (May 15, 1996): p. 10. Describing Mitchell in an impressive 54 column inches as "the poet of the waterfront," Severo offers in capsule a lucid and coherent profile-cum-obituary of the author.

Sims, Norman. "Joseph Mitchell and the *New Yorker* Nonfiction Writers." In *Literary Journalism in the Twentieth Century,* ed. Norman Sims. Oxford UP, 1990. An indispensable study of Mitchell's achievements from the perspective both of reportage and imaginative literature, based in part on several interviews with Mitchell. Sims uncovers some shaping factors in Mitchell's career not found elsewhere and wrings from his subject observations about his Fairmont days that appear almost verbatim in the "Author's Note" in *Up.*

Sims, Norman, and Mark Kramer. *Literary Journalism: A New Collection of the Best American Nonfiction.* Ballantine Books, 1995. Includes useful introductory essays by Sims on "The Art of Literary Journalism" and by Kramer on "Breakable Rules for Literary Journalists." A successor to (though not a true second edition of) Sims' 1984 book, *The Literary Journalists,* his text includes essays (one each) by Mitchell ("The Rivermen") and four other *NY* staff members (Calvin Trillin, Susan Orlean, Mark Singer, and Jane Kramer).

Sims, Norman. *The Literary Journalists*. ("The New Art of Personal Reportage"). Ballantine, 1984. Studies of Joseph Mitchell and a good number of other contemporary literary journalists, with a study of the form and an anthology (not including Mitchell).

Singer, Mark. "Joe Mitchell's Secret: The eloquence of a great writer's silence." *The New Yorker* (February 22/March 3, 1999): 142-150. Full page caricature of Mitchell by Al Hirschfeld. Singer, one of the most prominent of the current generation of *NY* staff writers, pays homage to a friend, a colleague, a mentor, a role model and an avid collector of artifacts. Having apparently visited Mitchell's home town in the Coastal Plains of North Carolina, Singer is enabled to understand how that environment played out in his mature work. Among those people that Singer treats in their relationship and significance to the writer are Dan Frank, Stanley Tucci, Marie Winn, William Zinsser, Philip Hamburger, and (most tellingly perhaps) Mitchell's beloved James Joyce. (Singer is well-suited for his present task as the *NY*: writer of the "US Journal" features once assigned to Calvin Trillin and now revived and assigned to Singer by Editor-in-Chief David Remnick. Singer's profile of Ricky Jay is especially masterful and worthy of the "Master"; *Mr. Personality*, Singer's 1989 collection of thirty-one profiles, begs comparison with the Joseph Mitchell's mature work.)

Skube, Michael. "New York Stories." *News and Observer* (Raleigh, N.C., August 16, 1992): 1G, 4G. Skube uses both interviews and photos well in telling this story of a North Carolina "native son" who made a name for himself far away from the Tar Heel state.

Smith, Stephen. "The Mystery of the Silent Typewriter." *New Statesman* (September 6, 1999): 29f. Having apparently read Mark Singer's article on the author (whom he had previously never heard of), Smith quixotically sets out in pursuit of this mysterious figure who he imagines once sat at the mythic "Round Table" at the Algonquin Hotel. He delves most fully into the relationship of Joseph Mitchell with two other Joes—Liebling and Gould—and he offers both a new story or two (especially the one about A. J. Liebling, Mitchell, and the "pecker bone of the opossum") and suggests a new clue or two to the solution of the mystery of the silent writer.

Smoller, Sanford. "Rosebushes and Bones: Joseph Mitchell's Enduring Values." *Pembroke Magazine 26* (1994): 10-31. A far-reaching analysis of Mr. Mitchell's work; Smoller suggests a number of parallels and/or influences on Joseph Mitchell's themes from such disparate canonical figures as Hawthorne and T. S. Eliot.

Story, Richard David. "New York Stories." *New York* (December 21-28, 1992): 98-100. Photo of Mitchell taken by James Hamilton showing the author among the rich detritus of the Fulton Fish Market. Based on an interview with the author, Story's essay is overly speculative about several matters in Mitchell's literary development and unfortunately quotes him as having said *"Ephiphany."* Story, does, however, induce from him that Reverend Brock in "Mr. Hunter's Grave" was a lot like Mr. Mitchell's father. And this comment from Mitchell: that Harold Ross was "somebody who may have acted kind of ignorant but knew a helluva a [sic] lot."

Streitfeld, David. "The Subjective Observer." *New York Newsday* (August 27, 1992): Part II, 60-61. Previously published in the August 13, 1992, issue of the *International Herald Tribune*. Streitfeld was able to solicit from Joseph Mitchell some distinctively heartfelt observations and opinions.

Strunsky, Robert. "Interviews De Luxe." *Saturday Review of Literature* (January 29, 1938): 12. A review of *Ears*.

Talese, Gay, and Barbara Lounsberry, eds. *Writing Creative Nonfiction: The Literature of Reality*. HarperCollins, 1995. Reprints "The Rats on the Waterfront" as the first reading in "Part I: Reality Researched." Other *NY* writers represented include John McNulty, James Thurber, and St. Clair McKelway.

Thompson, Ralph. "Books of the Time." (Review of *Ears*) *New York Times* (January 19, 1938): 21, 5. A significant early review.

Trachtenberg, Jeffrey A. "Bookshelf: His Ears Are Bent on Hearing Talk of Town." *Wall Street Journal* (August 14, 1992): A8. A review of *Up* which also offers a capsule summary of Joseph Mitchell's literary/journalistic career. Trachtenberg, however, seems narrowly focussed when he claims that the anthology "should be immensely appealing to anyone interested in bearded ladies, child prodigies, oystermen and Indian steelworkers." [But perhaps most of us are.]

Tyler, Francine, et al. "Guide to the Records of the *New Yorker*." In the Rare Books and Manuscripts Division of the New York Public Library. As plans were underway to move the offices of *NY* to 20 West 43rd Street in 1991, 2500 boxes of archival material (intra office memos, letters between editors and writers, annotated manuscripts, minutes from the weekly art meetings, editorial queries, and so on) were given to the New York Public Library and subsequently opened for use by the public in 1994. Without these records, such books as Thomas Kunkel's biography of Harold Ross and his edition of *Letters from the Editor: "The New Yorker's" Harold Ross* and especially Ben Yagoda's *About Town: The New Yorker and the World It Made* would simply have either been severely diminished or else untenable. Unfortunately, according to Ved Mehta's 1998 *Remembering Mr. Shawn's New Yorker*, at least 40 large boxes of material were accidentally taken to the dump. Mary ("Mimi") Bowling, Director of the Rare Books and Manuscripts Division, found that the records lost included "all the manuscripts and proofs for the first twenty-five years' worth of issues— from 1925 to 1950...." The materials relating to Joseph Mitchell in these archives date from January 9, 1935 (a letter from St. Clair McKelway suggesting that once the *World-Telegram* staffer has recovered from the Lindbergh trial he ought to do more "Reporters at Large" pieces), to January 24, 1944, in which William Shawn writes to Lt. Col. Marshall E. Newton that Mitchell has been advised by his doctor (a consequence of the severe attack of stomach ulcers that he suffered in late 1941 and early 1942) that he should not be sent to India as a war correspondent, Philip Hamburger being recommended instead. In addition to McKelway and later Shawn, other editors corresponding with and about Mitchell in these archives include Katharine White, Stanley Walker, and Harold Ross. A number of his earlier pieces were rejected, usually after some considerable revising and editing, but the staffers of *NY* were obviously placing considerable faith and trust in this newspaper reporter. Particularly interesting (in light of his later book-length profile of Hugh G. Flood)—and as well what became *JGS*—is a November 18, 1936, exchange. From Mitchell to McKelway: he tells McKelway that he is "working on a story about an inquisitive out of town boy in NYC, something on the order of a composite profile." On November 30, McKelway writes Mitchell rejecting the piece: "This Mr. Griffin doesn't seem to come up through this piece as a character at all." Fact and fiction have been "mixed up together with an unfortunate effect." Since Joseph Mitchell's great-grandfather's name was Hugh Griffin Mitchell and since he later attached these given names to his composite character of Mr. Flood of the Fulton Fish Market, and since in *JGS* he was to explore the embedded subconscious life of his early years in the big city, the links here are, at the very least, tantalizing.

van Gelder, Robert. "Books of the Time." *New York Times* (July 23, 1943): 15, 2. A review of *MWS*.

van Gelder, Robert. "Some Talk that Bent a Reporter's Ear." *New York Times Book Review* (January 23, 1938): VII, 5, 2. A sound early review of Mitchell's first collection.

Washington, Jim. "The Story Behind Joseph Mitchell." Photos by Steve Aldridge. *The Fayetteville Observer* (January 13, 2002): 1E, 2E. Relying on interviews with 82-year-old Harry Mitchell (Joseph Mitchell's surviving sibling) and Raymond Rundus (author of the then-forthcoming *Joseph*

Mitchell: Pilgrim in Manhattan) and on his own research and reading, Washington provides, in a leisurely 94 column inches, a profile in some depth and roundness of the Fairmont native who became a chronicler of the "lowlife" culture of lower Manhattan and an icon to his peers as a researcher and writer. The article is divided into an introduction and subtopics on "Fairmont," "New York City," "Joe Gould," and "Later Life." Of particular interest is a photo of young Joseph at about twelve years of age sharing a book with three of his siblings.

Wilkinson, Alec. "Setting the Standard." *Vogue* (August 1992): 156. Following up Calvin Trillin's comment in 1984 that Joseph Mitchell was the *NY* writer who "set the standard," Wilkinson seeks to demonstrate why his colleague at *NY* was the "great artist/reporter of our century."

Zinsser, William. "Journeys with Joseph Mitchell." *The American Scholar* (Winter 1993): pp. 132-133, 136-138. An incisive review by a former journalist who became one of the great rhetoricians and a mentor to numerous writers.

Ancillary and Corollary Sources

Abbott, Berenice. *New York in the Thirties* (formerly titled *Changing New York*). Text by Elizabeth McCausland. Dover edition, 1973 (originally published in 1939). 97 black and white photographs, with both captions and textual explications. New York is seen here in both in panorama and in the particular, with an enduring theme of entropy. Five of Ms. Abbott's photogravures were used to illustrate the sumptuous 1991 New York Limited Edition publication of *Bottom*. A detail from her November 26, 1935, silver gelatin print, "Fulton Street Deck: Manhattan Skyline," is used as a jacket cover photograph in the 2000 Jonathan Cape edition of *Bottom*. Diane Arbus (see "Bosworth," below) studied for a time under Ms. Abbott.

Adler, Renata. *Gone: The Last Days of the New Yorker*. Simon & Schuster, 2000. Adler, who was with the magazine for most of thirty years beginning in 1963, is convinced—and attempts to convince her readers—that *The New Yorker* ceased de facto to exist in 1987, when its brilliant, beloved editor and subtly despotic manager William Shawn (clearly a poster boy for the iron hand in a velvet glove mythos) was ousted by S. I. Newhouse, Jr., who took over control of the magazine two years later. Because her book is in large part a vendetta, Adler has a lot of bones to pick, and, when she shoves her chair away from the table, there is not much meat left on those bones. Nonetheless the book also serves (when taken together with doomsday tomes by Ved Mehta, Lillian Ross, Gigi Mahon, and Ben Yagoda) as a corrective to those who believe they are still subscribing to and reading the same magazine that was being published in the 1970s.

Anderson, Chris, Ed. *Literary Nonfiction: Theory, Criticism, and Practice*. Southern Illinois UP, 1989. As his title promises, Anderson has divided these seventeen essays into three parts: "Readings," "Generalizations and Definitions," and "Implications for Pedagogy." These essays derive most of their contexts from the moil and turmoil of academic discussions about composition and rhetoric in professional conferences and elsewhere from the 1960s to the mid1980s. The primary paradigms for the great portion of both theory and practice here derive from generative rhetoric, semiotics, speech act theory, and stylistics, with a couple of disquisitions being already tinged by the wide sweep of deconstructionism. None of the contributors seem interested in the literary nonfiction of any of the *NY* writers or of the literary nonfiction found in contemporary periodicals. The two articles herein that would seem to have most enduring value are Peter Elbow's consideration of Gretel Ehrlich, and Richard Selzer and Paul C. Hoy II's "Students and Teachers Under the Influence: Image and Idea in the Essay."

Anthony, Todd. "'Joe Gould's Secret'" is that there isn't one. But there is a movie...." *Sun-Sentinel* (Fort Lauderdale, April 17, 2000): n.p. The only review of the film which features interviews with both Howard A. Rodman (adapter and screenwriter) and Stanley Tucci (director and featured actor). Rodman (whose favorite quotation—from Samuel Beckett—"Every word is a stain upon silence"—mirrors a philosophical tenet common to both Goethe and Thomas Carlyle) deconstructs a complex truth in the relationship between Joe Gould and Joseph Mitchell and the writer's blocks they both suffered: "There are silences that are far more eloquent than some words. For all the work that Joseph Mitchell did, for all the work that Stanley Tucci did, for all the work that I did, there is something extraordinary about the fact that it is the power of what Joseph Ferdinand Gould didn't write that will bring thousands of people into movie theaters."

Applegate, Edd. *Literary Journalism: A Biographical Dictionary of Writers and Editors*. Greenwood Press, 1996. A pedestrian but disciplined and well-edited text—largely, however, as other reviewers have noted, redundant and superfluous, useful primarily as a place to start research into literary journalism.

Auden, W. H. "Writing." In David Lodge, ed., *20th Century Literary Criticism*. Longmans, 1972. Auden writes a candid and vigorous essay which "privileges" authenticity over either sincerity or originality as the primary mission of the writer..

Avila, Wanda. *Jean Stafford: A Comprehensive Bibliography*. Garland, 1983. Avila maintains that Stafford at her death in 1979 willed "everything" (not true, as Joseph Mitchell knew, when he pondered what to do with the books he inherited from Stafford) to "her cleaning woman [Josephine Monsell, ed. note]; Stafford even appointed this woman her literary executor. It is not clear whether Stafford intended this as a last gesture or as a very private joke." Stafford had also given Mitchell sometime earlier her "Henrietta Stackpole" rubber stamp.

Baker, Nicholson. "Deadline." *The New Yorker* (July 24, 2000): 42ff. Baker, a tilter at windmills as well as a novelist who treats erotic, bizarre subjects with narrative intensity (*Vox, The Fermata*) has taken on two Quixotic quests: (1) to save the print card catalogs of libraries (see his 2001 book from Random House, *Double Fold: Libraries and the Assault on Paper*) and (2) to retrieve paper versions of historic American newspapers (such as the *World-Telegram*). "Deadline" is an engaging account of his persistence and patience (and joyous but limited success) in the latter effort.

Bate, W. Jackson. *Samuel Johnson*. Harcourt, Brace, Jovanovich, 1977. Perhaps the best contemporary short biography of the great figure of the second half of the eighteenth century. The first journalist to put into perspective the value of newspaper work in relation to the "received" genres, Johnson said, "My other works are wine and water, but my *Rambler* is pure wine."

Bloom, Harold. *The Western Canon: The Books and School of the Ages*. Harcourt, Brace, 1994. The prodigious reader and masterful literary prophet, and our contemporary, finds *Up* to be worthy of inclusion in his "Canonical Prophecy for the Chaotic Age" (the twentieth century). The only other writers represented here with *New Yorker* connections are J.D. Salinger, John O'Hara, Edmund Wilson, Truman Capote, and John Updike. A. R. Ammons, a close contemporary of Mitchell's and reared some forty miles from Fairmont, is the only other North Carolinian in the "Canonical Prophecy."

Bosworth, Patricia. *Diane Arbus: A Biography*. Knopf, 1984. When she was just eighteen and a Powers Agency model, Bosworth was sent on an assignment to a photo shoot with Arbus. Thirteen years after Arbus's death by her own hand, Bosworth honored her with a forthright, thoroughly researched, and well-written biography. Joseph Mitchell is cited as among those whom Bosworth was "especially indebted to"—among the "close to two hundred people" that she interviewed or corresponded with in the course of writing this book. Mitchell knew Arbus's brother, the distinguished poet/professor Howard Nemerov, long before he became acquainted with her, Nemerov being mutual friends with *NY* contributors Shirley Jackson and her husband Stanley Edgar Hyman. Arbus apparently did not let Mitchell know that she was Nemerov's sister until 1963, three years after they first became acquainted. Arbus had initiated their relationship by calling Mitchell and telling him (as part of an initial two-hour conversation), that she would like to photograph some of the people that he had portrayed in *MWS*, such as Mazie Gordon and "Lady Olga." He eventually told her he approved of this project and, even though Arbus found out that "Lady Olga" (given name Jane Barnell) was dead and that Mazie did not want to be photographed, she continued to telephone Mitchell quite frequently from 1960 to 1967. The writer and the photographer shared some important interests, most of all a fascination with the lives of eccentrics and freaks, apt matter for their art. Arbus, Bosworth believes, adopted Mitchell's premise of a class distinction among freaks—those born being superior to those made—and Mitchell inspired Arbus's own "celebrated comments" about freaks: "Most people go through life dreading they'll have a traumatic experience. Freaks were born with their trauma. They've passed their test in life. They're aristocrats." (177). Secondly, by "hanging around" and being persistent, both Arbus and Mitchell were able to coax intimacy from their subjects and thereby to learn much of their needs and aspirations. Finally, both were able to uncover the keys to the inner lives of their subjects by much and ceaseless listening (in Mitchell's case) and much and ceaseless watching through the lens of a camera (in Arbus's case) until they would find the equivalent to what Eliot termed the "objective correlative" (Mitchell preferred the term "revealing remark"). One character they did portray in common (Arbus in the fall of 1960) was the pretentious poseur *Prince Robert de Rohan Courtney. In time Arbus would (somewhat in the same way that Jean Stafford placed her trust in him) tell Mitchell of her depression and discuss (in 1963) with him in a clinical fashion the act of suicide, an action she would take eight years later. They never met in person, but as with three other of Joseph Mitchell's friends and associates—Harold Ross, Joe Gould, A. J. Liebling—her funeral services were held in the familiar confines of the Frank E. Campbell Funeral Church. See also, above, the entry on Berenice Abbott.

Bryce, (Viscount) James. *The American Commonwealth*. Two volumes. New York: Macmillan, 1928/1927. Most likely the version read by Joseph Mitchell in the summer of 1929 as he was recovering from an appendectomy. Published originally in three volumes in London in 1888, Bryce's study of our politics—both at the national and the state level—is regarded by most historians and political scientists as second only in significance to Alexis de Tocqueville's *Democracy in America*. Reading Bryce's book inspired the young writer to head to New York where he thought he would become a political reporter.

Carduff, Christopher. Review of James Barbour and Fred Warner, eds. *Liebling at The New Yorker*. In *New Criterion* (February 1995): 73f. Carduff regards this collection of thirty-three previously uncollected articles as a "smorgasbord" that any lover of Liebling would be glad to own, but the sum of the editors' work is a "disappointment"—Liebling "deserves better."

Chancellor, Alexander. *Some Times in America and a Life in a Year at the New Yorker*. Carroll and Graf, 2000. Chancellor, a Briton residing in London who is a columnist for the *Manchester Guardian* and who has been a reporter and editor for several prominent British newspapers, was persuaded by his friend Tina Brown to come to New York as a deputy editor in charge of the "Talk of the Town" department. This he did from late 1992 until about a year later. In part inspired by the example of Brendan Gill's *Here at the New Yorker*, Chancellor's book is anecdotal, wide-ranging, and ample with names of the famous and notorious in New York society and in the more arcane nooks and crannies of the magazine. His exploration of some of the more popular watering holes and eateries (Grand Central Oyster Bar, Forty-Four Restaurant in the Royalton Hotel, and a number of obscure ethnic establishments) and clubs (Harvard Club and Century Club) within easy reach of *NY*'s offices added girth to his waistline as well as to his manuscript. Much of this book's value to those interested in crosscultural frissons derives from Chancellor's keen observations of American customs and values in the latter part of the past century. His observations about the fact-checking department at the *NY* (keying off from McInerney's *Bright Lights, Big City*), his comparison of Tina Brown to William Shawn, and his hiring of Jeffrey Toobin (which Tina Brown tells him is his "one enduring legacy") are among the most interesting of his insights into the culture of the magazine during a rather chaotic transitional period.

Connery, Thomas B., Ed. *A Sourcebook of American Literary Journalism: Representative Writers in an Emerging Genre*. Greenwood Press, 1992. Connery collects critical essays on 35 writers, from Mark Twain to Tracy Kidder, including an article by Norman Sims on Joseph Mitchell.

Core, George. "Stretching the Limits of the Essay." In *Essays on the Essay: Redefining the Genre*. Ed. Alexander J. Butrym. University of Georgia Press, 1989. Core, the editor of *Sewanee Review*, asserts that the history of the familiar essay in the United States can largely be traced in the *New Yorker*. He says that he "sometimes: believes that Joseph Mitchell is "the best of those [Thurber, White, and Liebling—along with Mitchell] who edged the essay increasingly closer to fiction."

Core, George, Ed. *The Sewanee Review*. Fall 1985. This October-December issue extensively focusses on the stable of *NY* writers of the first and second generations: included are articles by Seymour L. Toll on "Liebling in Paris," William Howarth on "E.B. White at the *New Yorker*," William Leary on "Jean Stafford, Katharine White, and the *New Yorker*," Melvin Maddocks on "James Thurber and the Hazards of Humor," and Gerald Weales on "Robert Benchley as Guy Fawkes."

Corey, Mary F. *The World Through a Monocle: The New Yorker at Mid-Century*. Harper UP, 1999; softcover edition, 2000. Corey's is a scholarly, readable, and forthright study of material from *NY* in the 1940s and 1950s. It ultimately will be of more importance to sociologists than to literary historians or researchers in literary journalism, as Corey's purpose is to describe and analyze how the magazine both reflected and attempted to deal with pressing social issues of this era. She cites Joseph Mitchell's "Mohawks in High Steel" ("an eloquent example of a tale focused upon Native American cultural agility") as an enlightened story about the Caughnawagas, Native Americans who showed enterprise and great skill in their work and in their contributions to enriching American life.

Cummings, E.E. "little joe gould has lost his teeth." In *E.E. Cummings: Selected Poems*. Ed. Richard S. Kennedy. Liveright, 1994. Included in the "Portraits" section of this anthology, the poem refers to the "Oral History" as a "wraith's progress." Cummings was one of the most faithful contributors to the "Joe Gould Fund" and one of his battered fedoras became headgear for Gould as well. This poem was read by a friend of Gould's at his memorial service in 1957. Gould's need for false teeth is a topic of the 2000 film version.

Daiches, David, Ed. "The Twentieth Century," in the *Norton Anthology of English Literature*, Fourth Edition, Vol. 2. General Editor M. H. Abrams. W. W. Norton, 1979. Daiches's introduction to James Joyce offers a keen perception of his themes and techniques.

Donaldson, Scott. "The Continuing Death of The New Yorker." *Sewanee Review* (Spring 2001): pp. 266 ff. A lengthy but rather thin, pedestrian, and derivative essay, primarily a hodgepodge overview of books by Renata Adler (Gone: *The Last Days of The New Yorker*), Alexander Chancellor (*Some Times in America, and a Life in a Year at the New Yorker*), Mary F. Corey (*The World Through a Monocle*), Thomas Kunkel (Ed. of *Letters from the Editor: The New Yorker's Harold Ross*), Ved Mehta (*Remembering Mr. Shawn's New Yorker: The Invisible Art of Editing*), Lillian Ross (*Here But Not Here: My Life with William Shawn and The New Yorker*), and Ben Yagoda (*About Town: The New Yorker and the World It Made*). One significant, inexplicable omission from Mr. Donaldson's kaleidoscopic survey (although her book was published in 1988) is Gigi Mahon's *The Last Days of The New Yorker*.

Ebert, Roger. "Joe Gould's Secret" (Review of movie). *Chicago Sun-Times* (April 4, 2000). Highly respected movie critic Ebert is intrigued by the Gould/Mitchell relationship in Joseph Mitchell's writing career and in the manner in which Stanley Tucci depicts it in this adaptation. He finds Mitchell to be the protagonist in the film because he changes and Gould does not. The film is "lovingly crafted…a chamber piece of quiet scenes, acutely heard dialogue and subterranean emotional shifts…. There is anguish here that makes 'American Beauty' pale by comparison."

Fenton, William N. Introduction to *Apologies to the Iroquois, with a study of the Mohawks in High Steel*. Syracuse: Syracuse UP, 1992. Mostly writing here a personal narrative of his involvement with Edmund Wilson on the primary research for this book, Fenton describes "Mohawks" as a "seamless piece of writing" and identifies the work of a professional anthropologist who followed up on Mitchell's stories about the Mohawk steelworkers of Brooklyn.

Fishkin, Shelley Fisher. *From Fact to Fiction*. Oxford UP, 1988. A brilliant, comprehensive study of journalists-turned-fiction writers Whitman, Twain, Dreiser, Hemingway, and Dos Passos.

Flanner, Janet. "Introduction: The Unique Ross" to Jane Grant's *Ross, The New Yorker, and Me*. Reynal & Company, 1968. Flanner's introduction redeems this book as significant to an understanding of Harold Ross (a "double paragon" as both an editor and a journalist) and of the magazine that he founded and prodded, pushed, cajoled, and urged into becoming the most significant serial publication of the twentieth century and the most influential magazine in the history of American journalism: even when compared to Henry Luce's *Time* and DeWitt Wallace's *Reader's Digest*. Ross's success in recruiting writers such as Dorothy Parker ("Constant Reader") and Robert Benchley ("Searchlight"), both from *Vanity Fair*, to write for the magazine were key early decisions. His own impeccable standards (he was an "unremitting reader" of *Webster's Second International*, and he made H. W. Fowler's *Modern English Usage* the "office book of law") may have left his magazine open at times to ridicule—as in Tom Wolfe's 1966 "Lost in the Whichy Thicket" article in the *Herald Tribune*, which made fun of the Rossian fixation—and thus *NY's*—with distinctions between "which" and "that"—but he also as a consequence of such valiant verbal militancy earned enduring respect and admiration for himself and *NY*.

Foley, Barbara. *Telling the Truth: The Theory and Practice of Documentary Fiction*. Cornell UP, 1986. There are two things wrong with Ms. Foley's title: there is very little "practice" that is given consideration (a Marxist professedly, Foley derives much of her discourse from such literary theorists of the day as Bakhtin, Althusser, Husserl, and Lukacs), and the book is concerned only with the "documentary novel." Tom Wolfe and Truman Capote are only mentioned in a single footnote and are not even indexed.

Franklin, Nancy. "Lady with a Pencil." *The New Yorker* (Feb. 26/ Mar. 4 "Women's Issue"): 172-184. A profile of renowned editor Katherine

Angell White which derives much from her relationships with Harold Ross, William Maxwell, Jean Stafford, Brendan Gill, Harrison Kinney, her son Roger Angell, and Joseph Mitchell.

Frus, Phyllis. *The Politics and Poetics of Journalistic Narrative: The Timely and the Timeless.* Cambridge UP, 1994. While she does not mention in this well-researched, cogent, and important study the nineteenth century journalists (Borrow, Cobbett, and Egan) who were so inspirational to both A. J. Liebling and Joseph Mitchell, Frus does in particular admire the work done by *NY* staffer Janet Malcolm and does pay some attention to James Thurber, E. B. White, Harold Ross, and William Shawn, and she also refers occasionally to Liebling and Edmund Wilson. She makes no mention of either Mitchell or Lillian Ross. In addition to Malcolm, the journalistic narratives of Stephen Crane (both the fictional and nonfictional versions of "The Open Boat"), the similarities and differences between Capote's *In Cold Blood* and Mailer's *The Executioner's Song*, other work and commentaries of Mailer, and several of the books of Tom Wolfe get especially careful analysis and interpretation. To Ms. Frus, the key markers that differentiate nonfiction novels from "true-life novels" (the latter especially becoming prominent since the 1980s) are "their immediacy, the research the writer has done, and her [referring here to Janet Malcolm] relationship with the subject." ("Preface," ix) Such markers could as easily, one assumes, be applied to distinctions between any species of nonfictional narrative in contrast to "true-life" narratives, a topic developed more fully and fruitfully by Norman Sims.

Gilbert, Stuart. *James Joyce's "Ulysses": A Study.* Vintage Books, 1956. A "new, revised, and slightly enlarged edition" of the 1935 text that aided Joseph Mitchell greatly in his understanding and appreciation of the structure and themes of the great novel by his beloved "JJ." Studying Gilbert's book prepared him for his meetings over many years with the James Joyce Society where it still meets today: in the second floor gallery of the Gotham Book Mart (Mitchell claimed to have read *Finnegans Wake* at least a half-dozen times). Gilbert also provided him with an understanding of the mythos of the cultures—both ancient and recent—that Joyce knew so well. Some of this understanding undergirds the narratives in *MWS* and in *Bottom* and even earlier inspired him to gather wool for the Joycean novel which was the context for the remarkable reverie in *JGS*.

Gill, Brendan. *Here at the New Yorker.* Random House, 1975. A welcome addition to earlier books on the magazine, such as Dale Kramer's and James Thurber's, this book by a frequent writer of "Talk of the Town" pieces and a theater and film critic for the magazine offers the reader an animated, somewhat gossipy, and overly self-referential (such as revealing some episodes of his own horniness) series of vignettes about *NY* folk and the folk tales about them. Covering a period of thirty years, it nonetheless provides an utterly invaluable and absorbing look (including some well-chosen photographs and illustrations) at the culture of the magazine created and shaped by Harold Ross, William Shawn, and their writers and editors. (Joseph Mitchell was a close contemporary of Gill's—both in age and in years of service at *NY*—and Gill had presented him in 1993 with the "Brendan Gill Award" of the Municipal Art Society for *Up in the Old Hotel*. Mitchell himself regarded *Here at the New Yorker* as an untrustworthy account and replete with mistakes.)

Goodman, Charlotte Margolis. *Jean Stafford: The Savage Heart*. University of Texas Press, 1990. A sympathetic and well-informed study, one which adds some additional insight into the relationship between Joseph Mitchell and Jean Stafford Liebling.

Gopnik, Adam. "A Critic at Large: The Great Deflater." *The New Yorker* (June 27/July 4 1995 Double Issue): 169-177. A retrospective evaluation of Thurber the comedic writer and Matissean illustrator, with Gopnik pondering the causes for his declining reputation. Thurber is compared at many points to E. B. White, and their contributing to the development of the plain modern style of writing (most notably in Thurber's 1933 book *My Life and Hard Times*) is linked to what Joseph Mitchell was doing in his early newspaper work: "he got there on his own at the *World-Telegram*."

Hall, John. *Fact and Fiction: The New Journalism and the Nonfiction Novel*. Chapel Hill: University of North Carolina Press, 1977. See especially Chapters Two, Three, Four, and Six.

Hamburger, Philip. "The Creative Life: Talk of the Town." *The New Yorker* (June 22/29, 1998: 42, 44. Hamburger salutes his and Joseph Mitchell's good friend, Al Hirschfeld (who died in January 2003 at 99), on the occasion of his 95th birthday. Together these three made up half of a convivial group of cronies organized by Harvey Orkin and disbanded at his death. The other two regulars (making up what came to be known as the "Deep Six") were S. J. Perelman and *New York Times* theater critic Brooks Atkinson—another source identifies Albert Hackett also as a regular. The group met weekly at the old Lobster restaurant on West 46th Street (Hamburger says it was on West 45th). Hirschfeld was also a friend of William Saroyan (who credited his reading of an essay by Joe Gould for freeing his writing of formal strictures) and a devotee of Gould's who contributed regularly to the "Joe Gould Fund." Hirschfeld, the theater caricaturist for the *New York Times* since 1925 or 1926, gained great personal distinction by being named a "New York Living Landmark." He drew caricatures of both Joseph Mitchell (reproduced in Mark Singer's *NY* article on Mitchell) and Joe Gould (reproduced in Judith Stonehill's *Greenwich Village: A Guide to America's Legendary Left Bank*). It would seem to most observers that Hirschfeld would have been ideally suited to be a prominent "artist" for *NY*. It so happened, however, that a whimsical cartoon he did of Harold Ross in the guise of Josef Stalin had done him in with the editor for that possible role.

Hamburger, Philip. "Foreword" to *Back Where I Came From* by A. J. Liebling. North Point Press, 1990. The long-time *NY* writer who came on board the year after Joseph Mitchell gives us an intimate understanding of his and Mitchell's colleague and friend.

Hamburger, Philip. *Friends Talking in the Night: Sixty Years of Writing for The New Yorker*. Knopf, 1999. While unfortunately lacking the convenience of an index, this collection of essays is nonetheless well-organized by broad topic or type and by chronology. The last two essays are posthumous reminiscences of Joseph Mitchell and Brendan Gill, both of whose careers at the magazine were encompassed by that of Mr. Hamburger, now affiliated with the magazine in eight different decades (1939-). According to Alec Wilkinson, Hamburger also provided the brunt of the formal presentations about Joseph Mitchell at the "*NY* Festival" in May 2000.

Hartsock, John. *A History of American Literary Journalism: The Emergence of a Modern Narrative Form*. University of Massachusetts Press, 2000. Paperback published in 2001. Praised by Norman Sims as "a substantial, well-written, and well-argued book that is likely to become a standard work in literary journalism," Hartsock's work is essentially a plodding historical overview of what he prefers to term "narrative literary journalism," and he takes every opportunity to sell that term to the reader. He is more interested in the theory and hermeneutics of the genre he has quite thoroughly researched than in its practice; Hartsock's writing, as a consequence, everywhere reveals his need for vitality and concreteness that might be exhibited at least in illustrative quotations from the literary journalists he mentions—and therefore ultimately the authenticity—that is usually the badge of the practicing literary journalist. He pays short shrift to both A. J. Liebling and Joseph Mitchell and fails to even mention any of the three nineteenth century literary and political journalists that served as exemplars for the "lowlife" themes of Liebling and Mitchell: George Borrow, William Cobbett, and Pierce Egan the elder.

Harvey, Chris. "Tom Wolfe's Revenge." *American Journalism Review* (October 1994): 40-46. Harvey postulates that, while Wolfe's advocacy for the "New Journalism" was weakened by an inadequate historical perspective, his prophetic instincts were so much on target that the elements of what is now usually termed "literary journalism" or "intimate journalism" or "creative nonfiction" are commonly used in newspaper and magazine reportage. Harvey regards Hemingway, Lillian Ross, A. J. Liebling, George Orwell, and John Hersey as writers who were already practicing "New Journalism" before Tom Wolfe. Harvey relies on Bob Woodward for a number of insights into current practice in the field, citing Woodward's *The Agenda* (about the Clinton administration) as exemplifying one practice now widespread in this genre: reconstructing of scenes or encounters, with no sources cited for the information. The alleged multitude of errors in Wolfe's attacks on William Shawn and *NY* in 1966 in the Sunday edition of the *Herald Tribune* are rebutted by Wolfe's editor in New York, Clay Felker, who told Harvey, "History has shown Tom was right. What they were doing [at *The New Yorker*] was embalmed stuff." Harvey also discusses the controversies surrounding Janet Cooke (the *Washington Post* reporter who was stripped of her Pulitzer Prize) and Joe McGinniss, whose 1993 book on Edward Kennedy, *The Last Brother*, recreated dramatic episodes in Kennedy's career without benefit of direct observation or even of interviews with the Senator.

Hough, George A., 3rd. "How 'New'"? *Journal of Popular Culture* (Summer 1975): 114-123. Hough takes issue with Wolfe's assertions of a "New" journalism and offers extensive evidence from newspapers and elsewhere as refutation.

Howarth, William. "E. B. White and the *New Yorker*." *Sewanee Review*. Fall 1985. Part of the special feature on *NY* in this issue: Howarth offers an incisive and informative portrait of a gifted writer, perhaps the most versatile staffer in the magazine's history.

Humphreys, Josephine. *Nowhere Else on Earth*. Viking Penguin 1999. This is a nonfiction novel by a well-regarded Charleston writer who has meticulously researched the history of the Lumbee Indians in Robeson County from the Civil War to the present day. The novel is narrated by Rhoda Strong, whose romance and marriage to Henry Berry Lowrie (Humphreys' preferred spelling) was part of the mythography of Joseph Mitchell's Robeson County culture. Henry Berry Lowry is the primary folk hero of the Lumbee people, and his and Rhoda's love is a central theme of the outdoor or symphonic drama "Strike at the Wind," produced annually during the summer at the Dial Amphitheater near Pembroke.

"Is fact necessary?" *Columbia Journalism Review* (Winter, 1966): 29-34. This article is a reply by Leonard C. Lewin to a letter written by Renata Adler and Gerald Jonas to *CJR* and includes the entire text of Adler's and Jonas's letter, a letter written to call into question the factual content (rather than the motivation) of Tom Wolfe's attacks on William Shawn and *NY* in consecutive April issues of *New York*, the *Herald Tribune's* Sunday supplement. (*See* under "Wolfe," following.) Lewin, drawing on Dwight Macdonald's using "parajournalism" to characterize the kind of "bastard" nonfiction that Wolfe and Clay Felker, his editor at *New York*, were producing and promoting, reviews the context for the development of Wolfe's attacks. He sides with those who reacted to Wolfe's articles as, in effect, blows below the belt of journalistic integrity and factual accuracy. Lewin's principal argument rests on the bedrock presumption that "Fact and fiction, like 'news' and 'opinion,' must be made distinguishable, however interwoven and however great an effort it requires from the reader or the writer." As a practicing journalist himself, his principal complaint is, "Where was Wolfe's editor when the copy came in?" Adler's and Jonas's letter, by inference and example, then, proves in exhaustive detail the soundness of Lewin's bedrock presumption and the validity of his complaint.

Jones, Malcolm, Jr. "The Timeless A. J. Liebling." *Newsweek* (November 26, 1990): 76. Jones keys off of Joseph Mitchell's eulogy at Liebling's 1963 memorial service to reflect on the increasing popularity of Liebling's work: "No modern writer makes better company."

Kempley, Rita. "Digging into A 'Gould' Mine." [Review of Film] *Washington Post* (April 14, 2000). Kempley describes Joe Gould and Joseph Mitchell as equally adept word smiths, one with tongue, the other with pencil and typewriter—with Gould perhaps serving as Mitchell's muse. As a "brainy, superbly acted buddy movie," Tucci's work "trumpets a marvelous paean to an increasingly endangered species: the word, whether spoken, written, or simply overheard."

Kerrane, Kevin, and Ben Yagoda, Eds. *The Art of Fact: A Historical Anthology of Literary Journalism*. Scribner, 1997. Both teachers of literary journalism, Kerrane and Yagoda usefully classify literary journalists into four categories: "Pioneers" (Defoe to London), "Telling Tales" (such figures as Hersey, Lillian Ross, Capote, Wolfe), "The Reporter Takes the Stage" (Orwell, Liebling, Mailer, Hunter S. Thompson, among others), and "Style as Substance" (Orwell again, Hemingway, Agee, Steinbeck, Wolfe again, Breslin, Didion, McPhee, and Mitchell, among others. This book comprises one of the most valuable of current resources in this burgeoning discipline. Yagoda makes a particular study of "Lady Olga" (the bearded lady) as exemplary of Mitchell's work: "What unmistakably marks the piece as Mitchell's work is its mixture of humor and profound sadness, with a subtle but insistent suggestion that we consider the particular facts under discussion insofar as they relate to the human condition."

Kinney, Harrison. *James Thurber: His Life and Times.* Henry Holt and Company, 1995. A massive volume of some 1238 total pages based upon interviews and research that stretch back over thirty years. Kinney, who worked as a reporter for *NY* from 1949 to 1954, includes a photo of Joseph Mitchell and credits him for providing a photograph of Ann Honeycutt. A biographical note states that Mitchell is "writing about, among other things, the Honeycutt/Walker/Mitchell/Addams group of earlier years."

Kluger, Richard. *The Paper: The Life and Death of the New York Herald Tribune.* Knopf, 1986. Kluger reveals some interesting tidbits (especially the circumstances of the inkwell throwing episode that resulted in the reporter's firing) about Mitchell's short career on the newspaper where he believed that he truly belonged.

Kolbert, Elizabeth. "How [Tina Brown] Moves Magazines." *New York Times Magazine* (December 5, 1993): 66ff. A penetrating interview of the new editor of *NY* and an analysis of the cultural and environmental changes she had wrought. Kolbert went on to become, after Brown's departure, a staff writer at the magazine.

Kramer, Dale. *Ross and "The New Yorker."* Doubleday, 1951. Not a strong profile of the editor or of his magazine. Kramer does suggest that the magazine let stand the fiction that Mitchell's Hugh Flood was a real person (see also Gill).

Kunkel, Thomas. *Genius in Disguise: Harold Ross of the New Yorker.* Random House, 1995. Karen Heller, in her April 1995 review, suggested that the energy and enthusiasm exhibited by Kunkel in his biography came about because Kunkel was "clearly smitten with his subject; [he} is as captivated by Ross as were those who knew him." In its larger strategy somewhat incoherent (Ross's second and third wives seem to be forgotten at times, and Kunkel seems not to know what to do with Ross's bouts of mental and nervous crises) but fortunately well-indexed, this most recent biography (which was nominated for a Pulitzer Prize) of one of the most interesting characters of the past century presents us with a three-dimensional picture of the man and his magazine. (See "Primary Bibliography" for more information about Kunkel and his forthcoming biographical study of Joseph Mitchell).

Kunkel, Thomas, Ed. *Letters from the Editor: "The New Yorker's" Harold Ross.* Modern Library, 2000. The acerbic and inexhaustible and endlessly interesting Harold Wallace Ross is well-exhibited in these "letters," only a fraction of which are addressed to staff members or to potential or established contributors. Reading the letters corroborates the opinions of some that Ross was, in the history of twentieth century America, one of its great personalities and one of the primary shapers of its culture. Kunkel in most cases both provides a context for each "letter" and identifies those named in these letters. Ross often candidly exposes his traits (some of them confessed shortcomings) in the earlier letters, such as to Dorothy Parker in 1927: "I'm nothing if not practical, and one of the leading men in New York although still in my early thirties." To first wife Jane Grant in 1928: "As for myself, I am a monstrous person, incapable of intimate associations." To Groucho Marx in 1929: "I am honestly unselfish most of the time, and not just an impractical dreamer—I am being eighty five percent unselfish in this." One might expect to find letters to his own staffers to predominate, but the variety of his addressees is quite astonishing; his favorite correspondents (in sheer quantity alone) appear to have been—along with the expected E. B. and Katharine White and James Thurber—H. L. Mencken, Frank Sullivan, and Rebecca West. He writes to Joseph Mitchell (about *Old Mr. Flood* in 1948 and "The Mohawks in High Steel" in 1949 [q.v.]) on three occasions in this collection. In a September 1946 letter to Hawley Truax, Ross also brings in Mitchell as he reacts to a note from James Geraghty regarding Charles Addams's complaint about not being reimbursed adequately. Ross: "Mr. Addams is a special problem, somewhat like Mr. Mitchell among the writers—excellent quality, low productivity."

Levine, Philip. "Joe Gould's Pen." In *The Mercy: Poems.* Alfred A. Knopf, 2002. Levine, who won a National Book Award in 1991 for *What Work Is* and a Pulitzer Prize in 1995 for *The Simple Truth,* has been acclaimed for the clarity of his poetic vision and for the passion with which he reveals and celebrates "blue collar" culture, which some would describe as the lives of the "proletariat." Levine, who grew up and was educated in Detroit, has spent the majority of his adult life in Fresno, California. His Hirschfeldian caricature of Joseph Mitchell is reproduced in Jim Washington's January 13, 2002, *Fayetteville Observer* article, "The Story Behind Joseph Mitchell." "Joe Gould's Pen," a first-person narrative, creates interest through the tension of its merging the form of a dramatic monologue with the tonal modalities of a reverie, and with the overlay of an indistinct sort of *apologia pro vita sua* (at times Gould's voice is heard, at times the narrator's/Levine's). In 140 lines of seven syllables each (with an occasional minor deviation), the speaker, who claims to be holding the pen that Joe Gould used to write his "Oral History of the World" and to have at hand one of the school books in which Gould penned part of his 9,250,000 words, ponders the magnificent failure of this historian's attempt to capture his life and the times in which he lived it. Four times Levine quotes from passages in the "Oral History" to illustrate how Gould's pen failed him. But, the narrator advises,

Don't blame the pen with its chromed
steel nib and fat black plastic
body that for forty years
carried the dark lexicon
of the mystery of one
little man and missed the point.

The point, the narrator says, is that as soon as the pen wrote, "each earned word would disappear/the way the golden halo/goes when the dawn shreds the rose/into dust, the way a voice fades/in an empty room, the way/the pomegranate fallen from/the tree scatters the seeds of/its resurrection, the way/these lines are vanishing now."

Liebmann, Lisa. "Guy's in the Hood." Review of Guy Trebay's *In the Place to Be. Artforum* (Nov. 1995): 15-16. Liebmann suggests that Trebay's essays (collected here from pieces written in the *Village Voice* from 1981 to 1993) owe much to Joseph Mitchell's *Up in the Old Hotel.*

Lounsberry, Barbara. *The Art of Fact: Contemporary Artists of Nonfiction.* Greenwood Press, 1990. Chapters on Gay Talese, Tom Wolfe, Joan Didion, John McPhee, and Norman Mailer. Useful bibliography. Indexed. This is one of the more highly regarded texts about literary journalism that have proliferated in the past thirty years; that is, since the publication of Wolfe and Johnson's *The New Journalism* (1973).

McGrath, Charles. "The Ross Years In *The New Yorker.*" 70th Anniversary Issue (February 20 and 27, 1995): 180-190. The new editor of the *New York Times Book Review* (and at one time a likely successor to William Shawn as Editor of *NY)* suggests that the aggressively anti-intellectual stance of the early *NY* resulted in the two prevailing themes of the magazine in its early days: how hard it was to get the magazine out, and how much fun it was.

McInerney, Jay. *Bright Lights, Big City.* Vintage Paperback, 1987. On the order of a roman à clef and written in the unusual narrative voice of the second person, McInerney's novel refers frequently to his chaotic workaday schedule at *NY* as a fact-checker. In that job, he evidently lacked the qualities said necessary for it: "a mind like a steel mousetrap and a heart like a twelve-minute egg." Among the *NY* staffers found thinly disguised in his story are William Shawn ("the Druid"), Eleanor Gould Packard ("Mrs. Bender, the senior grammarian"), and Joseph Mitchell ("the Ghost"), described thus by the narrator: "one mystery man up there [on the next floor]…has been working on an article for seven years." McInerney casts as the head of the "Department of Factual Verification" a woman named Clara Tillinghast, while the actual head of the department in McInerney's time would have been Martin Baron, whom Alexander Chancellor characterizes in *Some Times in America.*

Mahon, Gigi. *The Last Days of the New Yorker.* McGraw-Hill, 1988. This book is an authoritative and often compelling account of the circumstances that led up to the purchase of *NY* by S. I. Newhouse, Jr., the climactic event occurring on Monday, January 12, 1987, with the firing of William Shawn, who had himself served on the magazine's Board of Directors from 1951-1962. A year before letting the revered editor go and as he accepted the Henry Johnson Fisher Award from the Magazine Publishers Association, Newhouse had named Shawn as one of the three journalists with whom the successes and failures of his life had been shared. He noted that Harold Brodkey had called Shawn "a combination of Napoleon and St. Francis of Assisi, and I believe that too." In her "Prologue" Mahon (who characterizes Shawn as an "iron mouse") profiles the headquarters of *NY*, "showing its quaint old-fashioned style and endemic unfriendliness…." And, in a statement covertly suggesting Joseph Mitchell (p. 20), Mahon writes that "around half of the nonfiction writers took advances in the form of a weekly paycheck…. [The system] worked less well when writers became too comfortable, even lazy, and exploited the system by taking five or ten or fifteen years to finish an article." Mahon's view of the magazine as having in effect come to an end in 1987 in its historic role as a shaper and mover is reflected in subsequent books by Ben Yagoda and Renata Adler and to a lesser extent by those of Ved Mehta and Lillian Ross.

Mehta, Ved. *Remembering Mr. Shawn's New Yorker.* The eighth in a series of autobiographical volumes, all comprised under the rubric "Continents of Exile." The Overlook Press, 1998. Mehta, among the most profoundly intellectual of *NY* staffers, provides an intimate account of William Shawn and his family and the interior operations of the magazine. As Mehta was waiting after Sisyphean labors for the final disposition of his long and brilliant article on Oxford philosophy, he is led to lament, "Was anything ever done with at *The New Yorker*?" Mehta's uncanny memory (perhaps sharpened, like Milton's, because of his being blind) permits us to share with him in some memorable reminiscences of Joseph Mitchell: (1) Mitchell tells him that he would not have moved to *NY* from the *World-Telegram* if he would have had to be on a drawing account; (2) he tells Mehta that the common notion that Harold Ross was a "kind of a rube" was a pose something like that used by con-men poker players in Mark Twain; (3) Mehta says that Mitchell was the "office authority on fish"; (4) at a dinner Mehta gives for the Mitchells and Lieblings (Jean Stafford was now married to Liebling), Mehta is taken by the heady discussion between Liebling and Mitchell about Joyce and Hemingway and takes great comfort in "watching" the Mitchells dance to a series of Gershwin tunes played on his phonograph.

Mitchell, Therese. Photographic exhibit at Municipal Art Society, April-May, 2000. Therese Mitchell's photographs (including many candid images of street scenes and of family and friends) were kept in storage after her death in 1980. A number of them complement her husband's *NY* pieces. The 2000 Tucci/Rodman adaptation of *JGS* gives considerable emphasis to her work (she is played by Hope Davis) as a photographer. It is unlikely that Mr. Mitchell would have approved the depiction of members of his family in this film adaptation. His only reference in his writings, in fact, to Therese comes in the "reverie" passage in *JGS*, in which he refers to the "Scandinavian girl he has met in the city, and she is so different from the girls he has known in the South that she seems mysterious to him, just as the city seems mysterious; the girl and the city are all mixed up in his mind." In their preparations for the film, however, Stanley Tucci and Howard Rodman did seek and receive the cooperation of both Nora and Elizabeth Mitchell as well as of Sheila McGrath, Mr. Mitchell's longtime companion and literary assistant. Therese may also be intended in his reference to the "girl" he is dating who asks him, in the 1938 *NY* piece, "The Cave Dwellers," to let her go with him to see the Hollinans in order to give them the eighty-five dollars in donations generated by his newspaper story about their homelessness.

Newfield, Jack. "The 'Truth' about Objectivity and the New Journalism." in Charles C. Flippen, ed., *Liberating the Media*. Acropolis Books, 1974. While Newfield's critical acumen has been discredited in some quarters, his essay is pointed and resonant. Newfield, still an active journalist in 2003, disputes the existence of the "New Journalism," calling it a "false category." He also condemns Wolfe for, in his *New York* magazine account

of the New Journalism, never mentioning Murray Kempton, Jimmy
Cannon, I.F. Stone, A. J. Liebling, or "Joe Mitchell, who wrote for the rival
New Yorker. Like any faithful Boswell, Wolfe mentions only his friends.
[He]…is a gifted writer, but he has the social conscience of an ant. His
basic interest is in the flow of fashion, in the tics and trinkets of the rich."
(p. 61)

"*NEW YORKER* FESTIVAL: A Literary & Arts Celebration." As part of its 75th
birthday celebration, the magazine sponsored this first of an annual series
on May 5, 6, and 7, 2000. One of the highlights of this event was a round-
table discussion beginning at 11:00 a.m. on Saturday, May 6, on "The Life
and Work of Joseph Mitchell." The event was moderated by Dan Frank,
Mitchell's editor at Pantheon, and featured discussants Nancy Franklin,
Stanley Tucci, Alec Wilkinson, and Philip Hamburger. Mr. Hamburger
provided the greater share of the program.

Orlean, Susan. *Saturday Night*. Fawcett Crest Paperback, 1990. This second of
Ms. Orlean's books was published before she became a columnist at *NY*
(after Tina Brown assumed the helm). She is now a staff writer. *Saturday
Night* is built upon the premise that most Americans exhibit their most
extraordinary behavior while doing mostly ordinary things on this one
night. Each town or city in her chapters is chosen for one dominant activity, such as cruising, eating out, dating, gambling, bowling and so forth,
all of which come to illustrate one of her primary themes, which she later
termed "the dignity of ordinariness." She chose Pembroke, North
Carolina, 18 miles from Joseph Mitchell's home town of Fairmont, for the
topic of "Killing" and commits an egregious error (compare Rich Cohen)
by describing Robeson County as "hilly" when, as part of the Coastal
Plains, it is the home only of "flatlanders." Orlean, who has also written
for such magazines as *Esquire* and *Rolling Stone*, contributed during Tina
Brown's tenure at *NY* "passing scene" articles on such topics as sports,
music, and fashion and style. Her essay on Tonya Harding might be exemplary. Her worth and reputation as a literary journalist of stature have
expanded markedly in more recent years as witnessed by the twenty
pieces in her early 2001 collection, *The Bullfighter Checks Her Makeup: My
Encounters with Extraordinary People*, and the marvelous profile of
Automobile editor Jean Jennings in the February 19/26, 2001 *NY*. She is
also portrayed by Meryl Streep in the highly regarded film *Adaptation*,
based in large part upon *The Orchid Thief*.

Orwell, George. "The Moon Under Water." In Vol. III of *The Collected Essays,
Journalism, and Letters of George Orwell*. Ed. Sonia Orwell and Ian Angus.
Harcourt, Brace, and World, 1968. (Originally published in the *Evening*

Standard 9 February 1946.) Describes an ideal but fictionalized pub, six years after Joseph Mitchell's paean to McSorley's Old Ale House, "The Old House at Home," was published in *NY*.

Perelman, S. J. *Don't Tread on Me: The Selected Letters of S. J. Perelman.* Ed. Prudence Crowther. Viking, 1987. A diverse lot of letters from the hand of one of *NY's* premier humorists and a good friend and colleague of Joseph Mitchell's. (Brendan Gill, in *Here at the New Yorker*, reproduces a whimsical photograph taken by Therese Mitchell of Perelman and Mitchell walking arm in arm down a Greenwich Village Street.)

"Philippa's Day at the Fair." *Time* (July 1, 1940): 48. A story with photo about a nine-year-old genius (who has a black father and a white mother) that Joseph Mitchell visits later in the year; about her, he writes his only profile of a child. (For much more on the later history of this prodigy and tragic figure, see Talalay, Kathryn, following.).

Pinck, Dan. "A. J. Liebling, a writist at work." *American Scholar* (Winter 1998): 27ff. Using the techniques of the "New Journalism" set forth by Tom Wolfe and Norman Sims, Pinck recalls in this extensive piece his 1949 apprenticeship at *NY* under the tutelage and blandishments of a mentor whom Pinck found to be "exceptionally generous and sensitive." Pinck provides an insider's view of the working environment of the magazine: as Liebling characterized and exemplified it under Harold Ross. Pinck foresees a rosy future for Liebling's reputation as a writer about food, about boxing, and about the "low life" of New York. But "he was no journalist. What he was was an essayist of the first order: in the style, tone, wit, and scope of the learned, imaginative ingredients he put in the bouillabaisse of his pieces."

Roberts, David. *Jean Stafford: A Biography.* Little Brown, 1988. The best of three recent biographies of the troubled writer's career; Roberts is particularly cognizant of the important role Joseph Mitchell played in her life and in the life of her third husband, A. J. Liebling.

Rosenberg, Harold. *Saul Steinberg.* Alfred A. Knopf in Association with the Whitney Museum of American Art, 1978. A quite marvelous collection and a quasi-biography of the artist whom many would regard (such as Alec Wilkinson) as the greatest of the many great *NY* artists. Steinberg's link to Joseph Mitchell came most directly is his doing the distinctive line drawings for *Bottom*. But for a time he was also a neighbor of the A. J. Lieblings in East Hampton and thus also accessible socially to the Mitchells. Steinberg's life is as crazy-quilted as his art and nearly as fantastic (see Adam Gopnik's article about him, above). Steinberg traveled widely and soaked in a tremendous amount of imagery about people, animals, cityscapes, etc. Like Mitchell, his art bears comparison—in its offering meaning on several planes—to the writings of James Joyce. While seemingly blending together the techniques of a master draftsman with a Rube Goldberg sense of a "story" in his art (Steinberg described himself as "a writer who draws") and techniques often similar to those of comic book artists, James Thurber, or Pablo Picasso, this Romanian emigré, like Joseph Mitchell in his newspaper days, had amazingly diverse experiences: two examples are his covering the Nuremberg war trials as a war correspondent for *NY* (in 1946) and in 1954 following the Milwaukee Braves for several months on assignment for *Life*.

Ross, Lillian. *Here But Not Here*. Random House, 1998. This book has two subtitles, either of which are apt: *My Life with William Shawn and The New Yorker* (on the dust jacket) and *A Love Story* (on the title page). Ross's story is of the shared intimacies between two remarkable journalistic icons of the second half of the past century. While she spares us any details of their sexual intimacy (though it was real and transcending), her book is everywhere a chiaroscuro of their shared emotional and intellectual lives. Ross, an accomplished amateur photographer as well as writer, says that she joined *NY* as a reporter in February 1945 (at the tender age of eighteen, though her biography in *Contemporary Authors* gives the year as 1948) and became a staff writer three years later. Now in her fifty-seventh—or perhaps fifty-fourth year—and seventh decade—with the magazine (only Emily Hahn among the magazine's women writers has had a longer association, from 1929 until her death in 1997), Ross continues to contribute signed "Talk of the Town" pieces along with an infrequent longer article. When she was first interviewed by Shawn, she says that she mentioned the "marvelous writing of E. B. White and Joseph Mitchell and A. J. Liebling...." She would later learn that Shawn "reveled in S. J. Perelman, and he was sent soaring by J. D. Salinger and Ian Frazier and Joe Mitchell and Ed Koren and Roz Chast and William Steig." One of her photos that appears here (and also in Brendan Gill's *Here at the New Yorker*) pictures Liebling and Mitchell outside *NY*'s offices at 25 West 43rd Street, with this caption: "As far as I was concerned, Joe and Joe could do no wrong." A primary reason for the shared respect and intimacy among these three writers is that they all came to the magazine from newspaper reportage. Ross failed, however, in her introduction of Joseph Mitchell to Ernest Hemingway to bring about a mutual friendship between the two men, and her seriocomic narrative of this episode is one of the highlights of her book. Lillian Ross discovered another likeness to Joseph Mitchell in their physical act of writing: they both felt as if a "mystical power" was working with and through them as they wrote, and "[we]…would agree, while laughing at ourselves, that it was real." The most important likeness she, Liebling, and Mitchell share as writers, however, is their using the techniques of fiction writing to create enduring nonfiction.

Ryan, Maureen. "Green Visors and Ivory Towers: Jean Stafford and the New Journalism." *Kenyon Review* (Fall 1994): 104-119. A study of Stafford's "block" in the writing of fiction and subsequent work in prose nonfiction, which Ryan asserts deserves more critical attention than so far it has gotten.

Sayre, Nora. "The Frog on the Typewriter and Other Literary Visitations." *New York Times Book Review* (January 24, 1993): VII, 27. Daughter of *NY* writer Joel Sayre, the author, in this excerpt from *Previous Conviction*, recalls events of the 1950s related by literary friends of her parents. Included: an amusing anecdote about Mitchell and Perelman.

Sokolov, Raymond. *Wayward Reporter: The Life of A. J. Liebling.* Harper and Row, 1980. An excellent biography of Joseph Mitchell's closest friend and long-time *NY* colleague. Joseph Mitchell awaits his Sokolov. In his "Acknowledgments" Sokolov expresses gratitude to Jean Stafford Liebling for helping to open many doors for him: "The most crucial one was that of Joseph Mitchell's office at the *New Yorker.* Mr. Mitchell and his wife, Therese, knew Joe Liebling better than anyone else, understood him profoundly, and were gracious enough to allow me access to their collection of his letters." (Raymond Sokolov moved on from biography to become Art Editor of the *Wall Street Journal*).

Steinberg, Saul, with Alan Buzzi. *Reflections and Shadows.* Translated from the Italian by John Shepley. Random House: 2002. In the absence of a full-fledged biography of Steinberg (perhaps the most imaginative and provocative of the many great *NY* artists, his illustrations for *The Bottom of the Harbor* are perfect complements to Joseph Mitchell's mosaic style), this early record from the 1970s will provide a good beginning. (Steinberg died in 1999.)

Stonehill, Judith. *Greenwich Village: A Guide to America's Legendary Left Bank.* A "New York Bound Book." Universe Publishing, 2002. A nice supplement and a worthy complement to Ross Wetzsteon's *Republic of Dreams*, this is an attractive, well-organized, beautifully and aptly illustrated travelogue-cum-chronicle by a vice-president of the South Street Seaport Museum (which Joseph Mitchell worked to create), a longtime co-owner of the New York Bound Bookshop, and President of the Greenwich Village Society for Historic Preservation: another cause close to Joseph Mitchell's heart. The work of artists Edward Hopper and John Sloan (including one of his five renderings of McSorley's Old Ale House) and of photographers

Alexandra Stonehill and Berenice Abbott are especially prominent here. But Judith Stonehill also uses posters, caricatures, maps, and post cards to illustrate her text. One of the caricatures is Al Hirschfeld's lithograph of Joe Gould, and Stonehill offers a bemused thumbnail sketch of the author of "The Oral History of the World," who "was immortalized by Joseph Mitchell."

Talalay, Kathryn. *Composition in Black and White: The Life of Philippa Schuyler.* Oxford UP, 1995. This biography of the daughter of black journalist George Schuyler and his blond wife, Josephine Cogdell, who came from a wealthy Texas family, is uneven in tone and texture and somewhat perplexing as to what Talalay proposed to accomplish, but it is also the product of extensive and relentless research and gives us ultimately a layered and compassionate profile. Ultimately, in reading a life story so heroic and yet ultimately so profoundly tragic, we are bound to see the truth in an observation about Philippa Duke Schuyler by her Roman friend, Signora Cosi, "You know, God gave her everything, but she was very unfortunate." (230) And in an angry letter to her mother after her father had devoted five pages to profiling her in *The Negro in America,* she wrote, "I am not a Negro, and won't stand for being called one.... I had 30 miserable years in the USA because of having the taint of being a 'strange curiosity' applied to me." (224) Joseph Mitchell had reported on this "strange curiosity" in the August 31, 1940, issue of *NY,* shortly after Ms. Schuyler's ninth birthday. Subsequently, he and Therese occasionally paid social visits to the Schuylers. Though he spoke with Ms. Talalay on several occasions as she researched and wrote, *Composition in Black and White* suggests that she was not cognizant of the significance of Mitchell's interview with her—nor of the great popularity over the years of *MWS* (in which "Evening with a Gifted Child" appeared). *Composition in Black and White* is further enhanced by a number of well-selected and captioned photographs: from one of Ms. Schuyler at age two to a photo of her, now a foreign correspondent for the *Manchester Union Leader,* in Vietnamese guise shortly before her death, not yet thirty-six years old, in a US Army helicopter crash in 1967. The story that Kathryn Talalay tells is that of a young woman who eventually became much troubled by her biracial makeup and who was greatly vexed in young adulthood by trying both to please her mother and yet to escape from her discipline. She also was often distracted, yet gratified, by the contrary demands of careers as an itinerant concert pianist and an accomplished composer. She performed first in the Caribbean, then in Central and South America, then in Europe, and in her last years in Africa and Asia, a number of times in "command performances" before royalty and statesmen. In time she gave up her composing of music in favor of an often quite hectic performance schedule. In the last year of her life she began to follow in her father's footsteps as a practicing journalist (George Schuyler was a first lieutenant in World War I and made his name as a prominent black reporter and editorial writer). Philippa Duke Schuyler authored and published three books that are journalistic narratives and coauthored with her mother *Kingdom of Dreams* in 1966. She died in an ill-fated effort to resettle Vietnamese orphans. Her life's story, lyric and tragic both, would seem to provide more than sufficient matter for both a nonfiction novel and a powerful movie.

Theroux, Paul. "A Jolly Old Elf, a Master of Gloom: The Gifts of Peter De Vries." *New York Times Book Review* (December 5, 1993), 35, 38. This memoir of Paul Theroux's mentor and friend (whom Theroux regarded as "the most autobiographical of humorists" and "one of the greatest satirists of this century") served as the basis for the remarks that Joseph Mitchell, substituting for Theroux, made in New York at the memorial service for De Vries. Mitchell's wife, Therese, also knew the De Vries family quite well as she had taken photographs of their daughters.

Thurber, James. *The Years with Ross: with drawings by the author.* Atlantic Monthly Press Book, published by Little Brown, 1959. Begun as a series of pieces for the *Atlantic Monthly*, the book turned from a "common task of reminiscence" to an "ordeal of love." Together with Gill's *Here at the New Yorker*, we have about as intimate a portrait of the magazine in its heyday as we are likely to get. Most of the old-timers at *NY*, however, disliked the book. Wallace Shawn told Ved Mehta at his eighteenth birthday party: "He glorifies Ross so much that he scarcely ever mentions Dad." Edith Oliver, Shawn's "deputy" or "assistant" and quondam off-Broadway theater critic, spoke more bluntly, calling Thurber "a horse's ass."

Treglown, Jeremy, and Bridget Bennett, eds. *Grub Street and the Ivory Tower: Literary Journalism and Literary Scholarship From Fielding to the Internet.* Oxford UP, 1998. From the American perspective, Treglown's and Bennett's collection of scholarly articles seems not to be about "literary journalism" at all: unless the term can be expanded to include as its primary definition "journalism written about literature," and unless that loose and large genre could be restrained to focus on those institutions and those newspapers and magazines which have been instrumental in bringing attention to book reviews, literary and dramatic criticism, literary theory, and so forth. Such writers and authors as Coleridge, De Quincey, Virginia Woolf, such literary and dramatic critics as Lionel

Trilling, Kenneth Tynan, and F. R. Leavis, such academic institutions as University College London's English Department, and such serials as *Blackwood's Magazine* and *Times Literary Supplement* (*TLS*) we Americans would scarcely think to be at all relevant to what we across the water consider to be the shapers of, and contributors to, our more grounded and yet considerably more heady "literary journalism." Perhaps scrutiny of Treglown and Bennett's book proves yet again that Great Britain and America have endemic cultures that are separated by the same language.

Tucci, Stanley. Interview in "Playboy's 20Q." *Playboy* (September 2001): 135ff. Tucci discusses his ethnic background, his career as a director, his interest in the Thirties, Forties, and Fifties, his appreciation for Robert Redford's Sundance Festival (where two of his movies, *Big Night* and *Joe Gould's Secret,* have been shown) and expresses appreciation to Nora Mitchell Sanborn for her gift to him of a iron star fixture (used to support the walls of old buildings) from the collection of her father as well as "two silver spoons he used to collect from hotels that no longer exist."

Weber, Ronald. *The Literature of Fact: Literary Nonfiction in American Writing.* Ohio UP, 1980. Includes both an interesting Appendix on "Literary Nonfiction at the Decade's End"—in which Hunter Thompson's *Serpentine*, Norman Mailer's *The Executioner's Song,* and Tom Wolfe's *The Right Stuff* predominate—and a "Bibliographical Note." In the text of his book Weber's primary emphases are on Truman Capote, Dwight Macdonald, Mailer, George Plimpton, Gay Talese, Joseph Wambaugh, and Wolfe.

Wetzsteon, Ross. *Republic of Dreams: Greenwich Village: The American Behemia, 1910-1960.* Simon & Shuster, 2002. Although Ross Wetzsteon died in 1998, with the final chapter of this book not written, his thirty-two years as a contributing editor for the *Village Voice* and his passion for drama have served him well in the completion and publication of *Republic of Dreams*. This is a substantial (562 pages of text, followed by a "Selected Bibliography" and a mostly complete "Index"), although not definitive, history of the people, institutions, and events that made Greenwich village both renowned and notorious. Joe Gould is given a separate chapter, along with such diverse luminaries as Dawn Powell, Hart Crane, Djuna Barnes, Delmore Shwartz, Max Bodenheim, Jackson Pollock, Max Eastman, Edna St. Vincent Millay, E.E. Cummings and Dylan Thomas, William Carlos Williams, Thomas Wolfe and Aline Bernstein, Mabel Dodge, and "Jig" Cook, Eugene O'Neill, and the Provincetown Players. The chapter on Gould (subtitled "The Last of the

Last Bohemians") is based about equally upon Wetzsteon's acquaintance with Gould—and the contributors to the "Joe Gould Fund"—and Joseph Mitchell's two profiles in *JGS*. Among new information about Gould in *Republic of Dreams* is Wetzsteon's assertion that his funeral was paid for by the "Greenwich Village chamber of commerce" (another source gives that honor to the Lions Club of the Village). Wetzsteon also observes that Gould in his casket was "virtually unrecognizable" as his beard had been shaved off; and a Bowery friend of Gould's eulogized him by reading Cummings' "little Joe Gould has lost his teeth." Of interest also are the inclusion of two previously unpublished photos of Gould, both taken in 1943: one with Maxwell Bodenheim (whom Gould came later to detest) and the other showing him at his fifty-fourth birthday party doing the "Joseph Ferdinand Gould Stomp."

Wilkinson, Alec. "An American Original: Learning from a literary master." *The New Yorker* (December 27, 1999/January 3, 2000): 68-75. As Wilkinson wrote this tribute, he knew that his mentor and family friend (born one month later than Joseph Mitchell) was near death. William Maxwell, who had provided an introduction to the posthumous edition of *Joe Gould's Secret*, had also provoked and intrigued the young Wilkinson many years before at a dinner party when he identified Joseph Mitchell as "the best writer in America." Wilkinson also quotes—as he does again in *My Mentor*, his 2002 memoir and tribute to Maxwell—from Mitchell's presentation of Maxwell for the Gold Medal for Fiction (only awarded once every six years) to the American Institute and Academy of Arts and Letters in 1995, in which Mitchell compared Maxwell's theme of sadness at the heart of a family to that same motif in James Joyce's work and went on to assert that Maxwell "is as aware as any novelist who ever lived of what human beings are capable of." The comparison of Maxwell to Joyce is about as high a tribute as Joseph Mitchell could pay a fellow writer, for he believed that James Joyce was capable of writing in any mode.

Wilkinson, Alec. *My Mentor: A Young Man's Friendship with William Maxwell.* Houghton Mifflin, 2002. Wilkinson, one of *NY*'s best and brightest writers—as well as a contributor to *Rolling Stone, Esquire, Utne Reader, WE Magazine,* the *New York Times,* and the *New York Times Book Review*—has published books on a diverse set of topics and in greatly varied settings, including *Midnights: A Year with the Wellfleet Police* (Wilkinson served on Wellfleet's Cape Cod force for a year or so), *Moonshine, A Violent Act,* and *Big Sugar. My Mentor* is by far his most personal book: an account of his twenty-five year relationship with William Maxwell, the highly regarded *NY* editor and a gifted fiction writer himself. Maxwell, who died in 2000, was at first a neighbor and family friend, then a mentor to whom Wilkinson went at the age of twenty-four to learn the art of writing and the craft of publishing. He became ultimately and more importantly a friend and a father figure. Maxwell was an exact contemporary at *NY* of Joseph Mitchell's; it was from Maxwell's lips that Wilkinson heard for the first time the name "Joseph Mitchell." In a 1992 article in *Vogue*, Wilkinson—who by then had become an avid reader and rereader of the writings of Mitchell and had much of him by heart—called him "the artist-reporter of our century." In a recent communication, Wilkinson told me, "You would have liked Maxwell too. Mitchell did."

Winn, Marie. "Ruffled Feathers: A Bird's Eye View of Truth." *Wall Street Journal*. Vol. 228 (12/31/96): 5. Winn, who became a good friend of Joseph Mitchell's in his later years, observes that although he "wrote many great stories about New York City, only one touched even peripherally on Central Park...." "The Cave Dwellers" is a "hilarious account" of his encounters with a couple who had spent a year living in a cave in the park. Winn, a Czech emigrée best known as the author of *The Plug-In Drug* (an early exposé of the effects of television upon children), retells the main features of Mitchell's plot as a context for her major purpose: to discuss a *New York Times* article about birdwatching in the park. Winn's article here anticipates her 1998 book, complete with maps and drawings: *Red-Tails in Love: A Wildlife Drama in Central Park*. Like Winn, Joseph Mitchell was a keen observer of feathered wildlife and also a collector of birds' nests (cached in the dresser drawers in his bedroom at home—treasures found during his frequent visits to Fairmont in his later years). Also in these later years he spent much time in Central Park and enjoyed sharing its attractions with others.

Wolfe, Tom, and E. W. Johnson, Eds. *The New Journalism: with an anthology edited by Tom Wolfe and E. W. Johnson*. Harper and Row, 1973. Somewhat polemical and by later and better standards too evidently an appeal to the glitterati, there is nonetheless much of interest and of value in this attempt to define and ennoble the practice of literary nonfiction as it increasingly supplants an outworn genre: the novel.

Wolfe, Tom. "Tiny Mummies: The True Story of the Ruler of 43rd Street's Land of the Walking Dead." *New York Herald Tribune* (April 11, 1965); and "Lost in the Whichy Thicket: The New Yorker." *New York Herald Tribune* (April 18, 1965). Reprinted in *Hooking Up*, Farrar, Straus and Giroux, 2000. Wolfe's attacks on William Shawn and the magazine he edited appeared in consecutive Sunday issues of the newspaper on which he was then a staffer, and for over thirty-five years they have been nearly inaccessible—and for that alone the researcher and writer ought to be grateful. While Wolfe's linguistic exuberance, his panache and inventive machismo, may at times appear contrived, overly cooked, or "just too precious," there is no denying that his forefinger and thumb were always sensitive and (mostly) accurate takers of the pulse of trends—and especially the excesses in those trends—in American popular culture. Wolfe's knowledge of the inner workings of the magazine, while not perhaps encyclopedic, is certainly detailed enough to convince the reader that Wolfe had done his homework. And the venom underlying his parodic lambasting of *NY* would have seemed to many to have been an apt and more than adequate payback for *NY*'s frolicsome (if you were in the *New Yorker's* stable), scurrilous, maybe libelous (if you were in the Luce camp) earlier profile, courtesy of Wolcott Gibbs and with the hearty backing of Harold W. Ross, of Henry R. Luce and *Time* in *NY* (the November 28, 1936 issue). Tom Wolfe, by cataloguing the stables of fiction writers attached to *Esquire* and to the *Saturday Evening Post,* adds a logical, evidentiary basis to his argument that William Shawn was the embalmer to a dead or dying institution. He does so by refuting a common claim or belief that *NY* was the most attractive haven—or heaven—for short story writers and for writers of longer fiction. Wolfe suggests (in "Lost in the Whichy Thicket") that William Shawn's "hardest task" as editor was trying "to preserve the literary style of Ross's *New Yorker*. The thing to do, of course, was to adopt, as models, the styles of men who had been working under Ross—the so-called Tiny Giants, viz., E. B. White, Joseph Mitchell, Wolcott Gibbs, James Thurber, A. J. Liebling, people of that sort." In presenting his notorious pair of 1965 satires to the reader in *Hooking Up,* Wolfe has added both a foreword and an afterword. In "Foreword: Murderous Gutter Journalism," Wolfe, by reviewing his development as a journalist, by tracing the advent of *New York* from the Sunday issue of the *Herald Tribune,* and by explaining the circumstances which led him and editor Clay Felker to decide to launch an attack on the incessantly dull *New Yorker* on the occasion of its fortieth anniversary, seeks to sanction and win sympathy for his verbal skullduggery. In his "Afterword: High in the Saddle," Wolfe offers a post mortem of the windstorm created in New York journalism by his two-pronged assault. He notes the attacks on his work by J. D. Salinger (most surprisingly), by *NY* regulars E. B. White, Richard Rovere, Ved Mehta, Muriel Spark, Renata Adler, and Gerald Jonas (the latter two writing in *Columbia Journalism Review*), and by such other major players of the day as Murray Kempton, Joseph Alsop, and Walter Lippmann. Those attacks were capped by a call to Clay Felker from

Richard Goodwin, a speech writer first for JFK and now for LBJ (Godwin kept reminding Felker that he was calling from "the White House") and finally by a two-part attack by Dwight Macdonald in the *New York Review of Books*. Wolfe closes his "Afterword" with a pointed reflection on a sentence in Renata Adler's 2000 book, *Gone: The Last Days of The New Yorker*: "[She] opened it with the portentous sentence, 'As I write this, *The New Yorker* is dead.' I tried to tell her that thirty-five years ago. I tried to save her decades of dead end in her career. What else did she think 'tiny mummies' and 'land of the walking dead' were supposed to mean?" A reader of this *apologia* by Tom Wolfe will perhaps conclude by thinking, "This man may with some justice be regarded as unconscionable, but he is also certainly unrepentant." (*See also* "Is fact necessary?" above.)

Yagoda, Ben. *About Town: The New Yorker and the World It Made*. Scribner, 2000. In its reach and grasp Yagoda's study, the first true history of the magazine, is remarkable and exemplary. It deals with the innate qualities and dynamic changes of the culture of *NY*, rather than primarily with those personalities—like Thurber, the Whites, Wolcott Gibbs, Harold Ross, and William Shawn—who contributed to making it a rousing success. A great advantage that Yagoda had over previous chroniclers was that he had ready access to the archives of *NY* in the New York Public Library, material only available in the past few years. Yagoda's purpose was to write a "critical and cultural history" which would analyze both the form and content of the magazine and their evolution and then to study the role of *NY* in American culture. Except for an epilogue covering the last dozen years, Yagoda is concerned only with the sixty-odd years of the magazine's history from its founding through the forced retirement of William Shawn in 1987. Both he (implicitly) and Renata Adler also in 2000 in *Gone: The Last Days of The New Yorker* (explicitly) take for granted that the magazine is no longer—and will not again be—the cultural icon and literary beacon it once was. Joseph Mitchell was among the staffers that Yagoda interviewed in preparation of this work, but Yagoda did not derive much insight from him about the inner mechanisms of the magazine. As he had gotten older, Mitchell became more proprietary about the magazine. Furthermore, he was distrustful in general of academic scholars (even or maybe especially those ensconced in departments of journalism). This was primarily because he did not feel comfortable exposing any events or circumstances that might be inferred as detrimental to the hard-won reputations or achievements of either himself or his coworkers. For another, he felt strongly that only the day-to-day practitioners of his craft could understand and value its workings. He told me that trust

among and with his colleagues was subtle, not easily attained, but too easily compromised or jeopardized. Nor was integrity always maintained by
his peers—certainly not by Brendan Gill, for example, in his all-too-gos-
sipy *Here at the New Yorker.*

Zinsser, William. *On Writing Well.* Fifth Edition, Revised and Updated. Harper
Perennial, 1994. A *vade mecum* that is a guide for the writer in all guises
and in all seasons. Zinsser's measure of Joseph Mitchell's worth as a
model is dead on, and his analysis of Mitchell's use of quoted matter and
of a mosaic pattern of organization in "Mr. Hunter's Grave" is cogent and
well-reasoned, even set against his rigorous standards for such work.\

POSTSCRIPT

"He was an essential figure in modern writing and in the history of the city."
—"Postscript," *The New Yorker*, June 10, 1996

"…I don't ever feel that I've come to the end of Joseph Mitchell."
—Alec Wilkinson, 1992

"BARE RUINED CHOIRS"
—Epitaph on Joseph Mitchell's grave marker, Floyd Family Cemetery, Fairmont, North Carolina

In his eulogy of Joseph Quincy Mitchell at his grave side services on May 28, 1996, Pastor Emeritus Thomas L. Rich of the First Baptist Church in Fairmont noted that his parishioner's death on May 24 of stomach cancer at Columbia-Presbyterian Hospital in New York had occurred 71 years to the day since he had graduated (not yet seventeen years old) from Fairmont High School. Pastor Rich named the six classmates that yet survived. And he recalled the visit that young Joseph, then ten years old, had made to New York City with his father. (A highlight of this trip was a visit to the famous Ziegfeld Follies.) On his return to Fairmont, young Joseph confidently declared, "This is the place for me."

Although he (and with his wife Therese until her death in 1980 and later with their daughters Nora and Elizabeth) typically spent some weeks every year in Robeson County, the great metropolis, from October 1929 (he arrived just four days before the great stock market crash that marked the beginning of the "Great Depression") until his death, was his primary home. Later in 1996 other remembrances and memorials for Joseph Mitchell took place in Manhattan. Perhaps the most poignant of these was the program organized for October 2, 1996, at the Century Club, within easy walking distance of Mitchell's *New Yorker* office on West 43rd Street. Mitchell had been a member of the Century Association for many years, and this was the club where he often had entertained his out-of-town guests. Among those making remarks at this very special event were Tina Brown, Susan DiSesa (his editor at Modern Library), Brendan Gill, William Maxwell (who read from "Mazie"), and Philip Hamburger.

Several months even before his memory was honored at the Century Club, another significant memorial took place which probably would have pleased and embarrassed him in about equal proportions. Robust indeed in the "Postscript" feature in the June 10, 1996, issue of *The New Yorker* was the outpouring of affection and appreciation from his colleagues, both veterans (Maxwell, Gill, Roger Angell, Lillian Ross, and Hamburger) and journeymen (Calvin Trillin, Mark Singer, Janet Malcolm, and Nancy Franklin). Perhaps the transcendent emotion overarching these remarks was best expressed by Janet Malcolm, who wrote, "If there was an unkind word ever spoken about Joe, the person who uttered it must have been mad or thinking of someone else."

Most astonishingly, in light of this unprecedented recognition by and in *The New Yorker*, one simple fact stands out: it had been 32 years since Joseph Mitchell had published an article in the magazine. Yet he continued to keep his office and draw a salary. In any other context in the business or the corporate world that one can think of—the great exemplar in American literature is Melville's "Bartleby the Scrivener"—the coworkers or managers of such a "slacker" (unless perhaps he might be the owner's or CEO's near relative) would be up in arms, and a pink slip would be doled out most expeditiously. There were two significant reasons why Mitchell was able to enjoy such an unusual dispensation: the unique "corporate culture" of the magazine itself and the enormous reservoir of goodwill and respect that he had accumulated among the writers and editors during the 58 years he spent with *The New Yorker*.

Part of the secret of the enormous respect he had garnered from colleagues at the magazine derived from his circumspection about the workaday woes of these writers and the tribulations of their private lives. This explains his chagrin when he would talk about Gill's *Here at the New Yorker* (an act of betrayal at many points, Mitchell thought) and his reluctance to share information or judgments about his colleagues' work with outsiders, especially those from the academic world. As with other of the writers, he considered the magazine a "very difficult place to work" and felt his rapport with his peers had to be "maintained very subtly." Another reason for the respect he had garnered is that he took a great and genuine interest in the working lives and the achievements of his colleagues, especially those new to the magazine. Mark Singer was awed, in his first lengthy conversation with this venerable and venerated writer, whom he had first encountered in classes at Yale with William Zinsser, to find that Mitchell had been reading *his* work and would listen carefully, appreciatively, and enthusiastically ("Yehzz! Yehzz! Ah know it! Ah know it!" were locutions common to Mitchell's idiolect) to what Singer had to say about his own work and that of others that they both appreciated.

For a long time, as she enjoyed casual conversations with this courtly elderly gentleman (he introduced himself simply as "Joe") in the hallways of *The New Yorker*, Mindy Aloff did not realize what an iconic figure Mitchell was at the magazine. But this came home to her when she saw staff writers and other employees stand in line at his office door in 1992 with copies of *Up in the Old Hotel* in hand, hoping to secure Mitchell's personal inscription.

Calvin Trillin, who dedicated *Killings* to Mitchell as the writer on the magazine who had "set the standard," often marveled, in speaking or writing about his colleague, as to how this writer was such a skilled craftsman that he was able to "take the marks of writing off the page." Others have commented on the self-effacement of the writer/narrator in most of his stories: even when (as in, for example, "Up in the Old Hotel" and "Mr. Hunter's Grave") Mitchell's role as narrator-interlocutor might seem central. His presence is more obvious, though not annoyingly intrusive, in the newspaper reportage collected in *My Ears Are Bent*, and most particularly in the remarkably candid and forthright introductory essay, also titled "My Ears Are Bent."

Joseph Mitchell's closest friend and ally on the magazine, and eventually his and Therese's neighbor in Greenwich Village, A. J. Liebling, and Liebling's third wife, Jean Stafford, both left their personal libraries to Mitchell. Stafford, who knew how her husband detested rabbis and how Mitchell also distrusted evangelicals of most every rank and stripe (an exception being *Father Divine), still could teasingly but affectionately refer to the often gloomy-countenanced but always well-dressed Mitchell (Brooks Brothers suits, fedora in winter, dressy straw hat in summer, highly-polished leather shoes) as "Preacher." And in times of personal troubles or emotional distress (usually intensified by her drinking), she would call upon Joseph Mitchell (and Therese) to come to her rescue. Mitchell's colleagues remembered his loyalty to and his caring for the Lieblings.

His colleagues also recognized and were grateful that Mitchell did not have the preening ego of a number of better-known authors, those who had aggressively carved out "images" of themselves to flaunt in the media, in readings and book signings, and in "personal appearances." In "My Ears Are Bent" he is eloquent on his distaste for any form or degree of pretentiousness. Neither did he seek—nor would he have enjoyed—the status of being a "celebrity." Having been himself an interviewer, he neither sought to give interviews nor did he grant them—except in very rare occasions. He would not talk about what he was presently writing, except perhaps to say, "I'm working on a little something, but it won't be ready for a while." He would not give lectures nor even read publicly from his work. He would not accept honorary degrees. He cited Ralph Ellison to me as an example of what he wished to avoid. Ellison, until after his death (when *Juneteenth* finally came out), had essentially a claim to fame only with his first published work, the remarkable *Invisible Man* (1953). When Mitchell paid a visit to Ellison's New York apartment, he noticed a closet seemingly full of academic regalia, souvenirs of the many honorary degrees Ellison had been granted by colleges and universities. In July 1993 Joseph Mitchell visited Pembroke State University, which is about eighteen miles from Fairmont and an institution for whose Native American history he had enormous respect: his father would take him to its library to speak to Mary Livermore, a memorable woman and a distinguished head librarian. When the Provost offered him an honorary position as "writer-in-residence" or an honorary degree from Pembroke State University, he courteously but firmly declined.

Caught up in the overwhelming outpouring of respect and adulation that accompanied the publication and distribution of *Up in the Old Hotel* in the summer of 1992, his quiet and nearly anonymous world changed, and Joseph Mitchell's life was recharged with purpose and enthusiasm. It was as if the dam confining his long silence had held under water his reluctance to talk or write about himself and his endeavors. Now that dam had been breached, and it could not be replaced. He told me in a conversation in mid-1993, "I feel like a washing machine."

It was not that he had not been keeping busy. And he could also have said, as Joe Gould did after Mitchell had berated him for being lazy for not having written the "Oral History," "It's not a question of laziness." Besides the extensive writing that he seemingly was doing in his office all these years that may yet appear in print, Joseph Mitchell actually did considerable and verifiable writing and rewriting in the last few years of his life. He worked for a number of years on the masterful "Author's Note" of 2,000 or more words that prefaced the 1992 anthology. With some assistance from his companion and literary assistant, Sheila McGrath, he added about the same number of words to "The Old House at Home," and he revised considerably the ending of "A Spism and a Spasm." Later he would do the flap copy for the Modern Library editions of *Ears* and *MWS*, and he made kind of a hobby of designing and writing the words on tombstones, especially seen in the care and time he took with Therese's grave marker and then his own, each involving a quotation from a sonnet by Shakespeare. He did, however, turn down a suggestion from Tina Brown that he write something for the magazine about the fire that devastated a good portion of his beloved Fulton Fish Market. (Ironically, a few years after his death, much of the "Mitchell Warehouse" in Fairmont was also devastated by fire. It was his comparison of the fish market on Water Street to the Border Belt Tobacco Market and the warehouse activity in Fairmont that was supposedly one of the books that he was working on in his later years.)

Then there was the not inconsiderable burden on his time, talents, and energies that his increased involvement in civic affairs required, activities that took him away from his *New Yorker* office. He served from 1972 to 1980 on the very important South Street Seaport Museum Restoration Committee, a task which extended in part to the revitalization of a large area near the Fulton Fish Market. He also served as an appointee of Mayor Ed Koch to a five-year term from 1982 to 1987 on the New York Landmarks Preservation Commission. He also continued memberships in several other organizations, and he regularly attended meetings of the James Joyce Society upstairs in the Gotham Book Mart (where it still meets today). A lifelong devotee of his beloved "JJ," he claimed to have read *Finnegans Wake* at least a half-dozen times. A member of the American Academy and Institute of Arts and Letters since 1959, he also served terms in that illustrious institution as treasurer and vice president. Close friends with one of the senior ministers at Grace (Episcopal) Church, which he regarded as his favorite institution in New York City, he served as its vestryman. He spent more time in his later years in Central Park, and he continued to enjoy his hobbies of learning about wild flowers, birds and their nests, the scroll work and cast iron art of old buildings, eating and drinking in his favorite establishments in Greenwich Village and elsewhere, placing his wagers on the Irish Sweepstakes, and so on. He also visited the British Isles after the clamor of dealing with the demands placed on him by the success of *Up* had diminished.

Because of circumstances in family matters, he also began spending more time in Fairmont and the surrounding area. Therese had died in Fairmont in 1980, and he had seen to her burial in a plot near that of his parents in the Floyd Family Cemetery on the northwestern edge of Fairmont. Earlier than this event, he had at his mother's death in 1963 inherited two farms in the Parker heritage and then at his father's death in 1976 he inherited with his five siblings a share of the 3500 acres of land that his father owned. He became interested and involved in the techniques of modern farming and more especially in reforestation efforts in that part of his inheritance that lay in the Ashpole Swamp area, a domain which he named "Fox Bay," and to which he refers memorably in the "Author's Note" to *Up in the Old Hotel.*

Therefore, we should not perhaps be surprised to realize that even a writer of Joseph Mitchell's stature, once removed so nearly completely and so long from public scrutiny, could be forgotten. From December 1965, when his good friend Stanley Edgar Hyman's "The Art of Joseph Mitchell" appeared in the quite obscure *New Leader*, until the Spring 1983 issue of *Sewanee Review*, when Noel Perrin's "Joseph Mitchell: Paragon of Reporters" appeared, nothing but ephemera was printed about him. And all of his books by that time had been out of print for many years. From 1983 to 1992, except for a brief squib in *New York* in February 1987 about his intention of bringing forth an "omnibus volume," nothing further of any consequence appeared in the periodical press or elsewhere. He had refused persistently to permit any of his books to be released in new paperback editions, and he would seldom grant permission to include his writings in anthologies or miscellanies. Many who had read his work in *The New Yorker*—and most of the new readers who had come across his writings in bookstores or in libraries—assumed that he was deceased. The only public recognition that came to him during this time was the North Carolina Award in Literature, given to him in 1984 in Raleigh at a reception and dinner for all honorees.

Joseph Mitchell did not anticipate the overwhelming response to the publication of *Up*. At times he would be embarrassed and at many other times would feel harried and frustrated by all the demands that, now that he was 84, made up each day. But he was also enormously energized. It was if the heavy burdens of the past (especially the ghost of Joe Gould) were being lifted, the gloom of his long silence was lifting, and the body of his work was being validated for new generations of readers. He would certainly be pleased to learn that the paperback edition of *Up* remains in print, and it appears it will so remain in perpetuity.

In my possession are some fifty-plus items that Joseph Mitchell so generously gave me in July 1993 as we returned to the family home on Church Street in Fairmont from a visit to Pembroke State University, now the University of North Carolina at Pembroke. The great majority of these are reviews of *Up* and retrospectives of his literary career, and they are from newspapers and magazines across the country. These reviewers unanimously greeted the anthology with accolades of welcoming pleasure. *Up in the Old Hotel* made several best seller lists; it was reissued by the Quality Paperback Book Club. *Time* named it the second most important nonfiction book of 1992, and it won both the Ambassador Book Award of the "Books-Across-the-Sea" program and the Brendan Gill Award of the Municipal Art Society. In short order both *The Bottom of the Harbor* and *Joe Gould's Secret* were reissued in editions under the aegis of the "Modern Library."

In a manner like unto that of the aged dray horse in *Old Mr. Flood* whose vitality and libido are revived by a daily diet of oysters, Joseph Mitchell first acknowledged, then began to enjoy, even revel in, giving interviews—in his office, in McSorley's Old Ale House, even sitting in strange places for radio and television programs. When he finally began talking openly about his long silence and his troubled, even destructive relationship with Joe Gould, he could hardly stop. He even went back to Chapel Hill—still lacking completion of math and chemistry requirements—in 1993 where he was granted the great distinction of being named a "Bicentennial Distinguished Alumnus." BBC Radio in late 1992 did a series of programs using eight abridged versions of his *MWS* stories with the distinguished actor Eli Wallach performing. The Modern Library editions were reprinted in England by Jonathan Cape, and more translations began to appear, especially of *JGS*. On February 6, 1996, not long before his death on May 24, 1996, Joseph Mitchell did his first public reading, at Books & Co. (since closed), from the Modern Library edition of *JGS*. Those who could not get inside through the crowd milled around outside on the sidewalk until the reading was over.

The two most important events related to Joseph Mitchell's career since his death have been the making of the excellent film adaptation of *JGS* in 2000 and the appearance in print for the first time since 1938 of a new, revised edition of *Ears*. Simultaneously with the latter appeared a handsome new edition of *MWS*, which has been and will continue to be Joseph Mitchell's most popular book.

Joseph Mitchell, because of his superb craftsmanship, will always be admired and emulated as a writer. As a creator of memorable characters, nearly all of them taken from life, he has created a tapestry of the human pageant that merits comparison to the *Canterbury Tales*, Balzac's *Comédie Humaine*, Charles Dickens' novels, and James Joyce's *Dubliners*.

What will distinguish Mitchell from all these other writers will be his distinctive temperament, his ability to merge the tragic with the comic, the heroic with the commonplace, and the lyric with the prosaic. Nearly every character that Joseph Mitchell wrote about can be used to illustrate one of more of these tensions that reside in human nature. As George H. Hunter put it, "Stones rot the same as bones rot, and nothing endures but the spirit." However, no anecdote that I have encountered more perfectly captures his distinctive sense of humor than one that Nancy Franklin recalled in the June 10, 1996, memorial tribute in *The New Yorker*. In a telephone conversation with him in January 1996, shortly after a great blizzard had struck New York (Franklin had been interviewing him for her upcoming profile of Katharine White), Mitchell told her that James Thurber, now become totally blind, was once told by his wife that it had begun snowing, and Thurber replied, "Oh, no, not another goddam fairyland." Mitchell told Franklin that it was the kind of observation that he treasured "because it said everything—or, as he put it, it was 'tragedy and comedy all balled up into one thing.'"

INDEX

Note: An asterisk (*) within the citations signifies that the topic indicated was of primary interest in a nonfiction article or book by Joseph Mitchell. Only those topics referred to in the textual material or in the "Secondary" and "Ancillary and Corollary" sources are so identified: refer to the "Primary Bibliography" for a complete listing of Mr. Mitchell's works that were published in *The New Yorker* between 1933 and 1964. Refer to both the 1938 and 2001 editions of *My Ears Are Bent* for his newspaper articles that were collected in one or both of these volumes . The italicized abbreviation *bib.* following a title signifies that this item is both listed and commented upon—on that page or those pages—as a separate item within one of the several bibliographies in this study: whether "Primary," "Secondary," or "Ancillary and Corollary."

Betjeman, John, 11
Big Sugar: Seasons in the Cane Fields of Florida (Alec Wilkinson), 63
Bigelow, Scott, 22*bib.*
"Black Tuesday" (October 29, 1929), 24
Bishop, Elizabeth, 23
Bloom, Harold, xi, 40*bib.*
Blount, Roy, Jr., 11, 22 *bib.*
*Boas, Franz, xiii, 2, 11
Bodenheim, Maxwell, 62
Boe, John (interview with Calvin Trillin), xxvii, 19*bib.*
Books & Co. *See* New York City
Borrow, George ("lowlife" topics), xxiii, 45, 47
Bosworth, Patricia. *See Diane Arbus: A Biography*
Boston Globe, 28
Bottom of the Harbor, The (Joseph Mitchell), xiii, xxii, xxviii-xxix, xxxi, 11, 13-14*bib.*,
    15, 20, 38, 45, 56, 58, 72. *See also* Mitchell, Joseph—literary preoccupations and
    themes
    editions of, 14
    reviews of, 14, 21, 25, 25-26, 29, 31, 72
    "Bottom of the Harbor, The" (*New York Harbor," *Archie Zimmer, and *Leroy
    Poole), xxv, 5*bib*, 13-14
    "Dragger Captain" (*Ellery Franklin Thompson and *Stonington, Connecticut),
    xxiv, 5bib., 13-14
    "Mr. Hunter's Grave" (*George H. Hunter and *South Shore of Staten Island),
    xxiv, xxv, xxx, 5*bib.*, 13, 14, 25, 27, 29, 35, 68, 69, 73
    "Rats on the Waterfront, The" (*rats on the New York waterfront, originally titled
    "Thirty-two Rats from Casablanca"), xxiv, xxviii, xxix, 13-14, 31, 35
    "Rivermen, The" (*Edgewater, New Jersey, and *Harry Lyons), xxv, xxx, 5*bib.*, 13-
    14, 33
    Noel Perrin on, 31-32
    strategies of opening sentences, xxx
    tensions created between fecundity and decay, etc., xxxi, 73
    "Up in the Old Hotel," originally titled "The Cave" (*Louis Morino and *Fulton
    Ferry Hotel), xxviii, xxx, 13-14, 69
*Bow, Clara, xiii, 11
Bowery. *See* New York City
Bowling, Mary ("Mimi"—*NY* archives), 35-36
Braswell, Laura Mitchell (sister and dedicatee), 15
Breslin, Jimmy, 22, 23*bib.*, 26, 49
Breughel, Pieter, xxiii

"Coffins! Undertakers! Hearses!" (second in series about *Hugh Griffin Flood), 8, 12*bib*. *See Old Mr. Flood*

*Cohan, George M., xiii, 11

Cohen, Rich, 24*bib*.(2), 55

*Colborne, Arthur S. ("Don't Swear Man"), xii

Comédie Humaine, La (Honoré de Balzac), 73

*Commodore Dutch, xii. *See* "Tooth, The"

Composition in Black and White (*Philippa Duke Schuyler), 59, 60*bib*.

Connery, Thomas B. See A *Sourcebook of American Literary Journalism*

Cooke, Janet, 48

"Cool Swamp and Field Woman" (early Mitchell story), 2, 17

Core, George, 24*bib*., 42*bib*.(2)

Corey, Mary F. *See World Through a Monocle*

Costello, Tim, xii-xiii, xxiii

Cottrell, Sophie, 12

*Courtney, Prince Robert de Rohan, 41

*Coward, Noël, 11

Cowley, Malcolm, xv, 11, 21, 32; "The Grammar of Facts," xxx*bib*., 24; first to appreciate Mitchell as a literary artist, xxx, 24

Crane, Stephen, xxiii; comparison of "Open Boat" narratives by Frus, 45

"creative nonfiction." *See* "literary journalism"

Critic's Credentials, The. See Hyman, Stanley Edgar

*Crosby, Bing, 11

*Cubitt, Florence (nudist queen and dancer). *See* "Mr. Grover A. Whalen and the Midway"

cummings, e.e., 2, 23, 43, 61; "little joe gould has lost his teeth," 43, 62

Daiches, David, 43*bib*.

Daily Tar Heel, 2

Davis, Hope (as Therese Mitchell), 28, 54

"Deaf-Mutes Club, The" (*Union League of the Deaf). *See* "But There is No Sound"

"Deep Six" (Mitchell a member of), xxiii, 21, 46

Defoe, Daniel, xxiii, 49

Denby, David, review of film of *JGS*, 24-25*bib*.

de Tocqueville, Alexis (*Democracy in America*), 41

De Vries, Peter, 16. *See also* Theroux, Paul

Diane Arbus: A Biography (Bosworth), 40-41*bib*.

"Diary." *See* Hawthorne, Mary

Dickens, Charles, xxiii, 21, 32, 73

Dickey, James, 32

Luks, George (painter), 30
Lumbee Tribe of Cheraw Indians. *See* Robeson County
Lynch, William S., 4, 30*bib.*
*Lyons, Harry. *See* "The Rivermen" in *Bottom*
Lynch, William S., 28, 55*bib.*

Macdonald, Dwight, 49, 61, 65
Macmillan, Bob, 19
*Madden, Joe, 4*bib.*
Maddocks, Melvin (on Thurber), 42
Mahon, Gigi. *See* *Last Days of the New Yorker, The* .
Mailer, Norman, 20, 49, 52, 61. *See also Executioner's Song, The*
Malcolm, Janet, xiii, xxiii, 45
Maliszewski, Paul, 3
Maloney, Russell, 19
"Man Named Me, A" (working title of Mitchell's autobiography), 16*bib.*, 23
"Marker, The" (*Joe Madden, saloon keeper), 4*bib.*
Martin, Steve (as Charles Duell), 53
Marx, Groucho, 51
Matisse, Henri, xxiii
Max, Daniel, 30*bib.*
Maxwell, William, xiii, xvi, xxiii, 14, 20, 32, 45, 62-63, 68
    Alec Wilkinson's reminiscences, 20, 62-63
    identifies Mitchell as "best writer in America," 62
    Mitchell presents him Gold Medal for Fiction for American Academy, 62
    writes "Introduction" to "Commemorative" Modern Library edition of *JGS*, 14, 62
"Mayor of the Fish Market" (first in series on *Hugh Griffin Flood, later retitled "Old
    Mr. Flood"): 4*bib.* *See Old Mr. Flood*
"Mazie" (*Mazie P. Gordon), xii, xxiv, 4*bib.*, 12, 23, 27, 40
McEvoy, Dermot, 12, 30*bib.*
McGinniss, Joe (*The Last Brother*), 48
McGrath, Charles, xiii, 30*bib.*, 52*bib.*
McGrath, Sheila (executrix, companion, literary assistant), xiii, xxi, xxiii, 11, 15-16, 54, 70
McInerney, Jay. *See Bright Lights, Big City*
McKelway, St. Clair (editor in early career at *NY*), xiii, xxiii 19, 36-37
McNulty, John, 35
McPhee, John, 49, 52
McSorley, John, xii, 4, 6
McSorley's Old Ale House. *See* New York City (Greenwich Village)
McSorley's Wonderful Saloon, xii, xv, xvi, xxix, xxxi, 11-12*bib.*, 30, 31, 40, 45, 70, 73

Personality and temperament, 23, 28, 29, 33, 68-70. *See also* 1996 "POSTSCRIPT" article in NY

Rhetoric of his writing. *See also* Carduff, Cowley, Hyman, Sante, Wilkinson (*Vogue*), and Zinsser

ambivalence in major themes, 23

catalogue as a distinctive trait, xxviii

"distressing overuse of quotations," 33

equivocal leads ("hooks") in story openings, xxx

"greatest living master of the English declarative sentence," xxix

fondness for "imagery in vulgar conversation," xxviii,17

"revealing remark" ("objective correlative") as key to stories, 41

JGS as a "paradigm of organization," 24

parallelism and use of coordinate modifiers, xxviii-xxix

rhetorical patterns in "Cool Swamp and Field Woman," 2

similes and metaphors from commonplace experience, xxviii.

Mitchell, Nora (daughter), xiii, 14, 16, 54, 61, 67

Mitchell, Quince Bostic (grandfather), 25

Mitchell, Therese (wife), xxi, 10, 12, 16, 54, 56, 60, 67, 69, 70, 71

career as a photographer, xiii, 54*bib.*, 56

dramatized in film version of *JGS*, 28, 54

exhibit in Municipal Art Society gallery in 2000, 54

Mitchell, (William) Harry (brother), 11, 15, 26, 36

Modern English Usage (Fowler: the *NY*'s "office book of law"), 44

"Mohawks in High Steel" (*Brooklyn and *Canadian Caughnawagas), xxiv, 8*bib.*, 13*bib.*, 15, 43, 51

Monsell, Josephine, 39

Moonshine: A Life in the Pursuit of White Liquor (Alec Wilkinson), 62-63

"Moon Under Water, The." *See* Orwell, George

*Morgan, Helen, 11

Morino, Amil, xxviii

*Morino, Louis, xii, xxviii, xxx. See *Bottom* ("Up in the Old Hotel")

"Mr. Barbee's Terrapin," later titled "The Same as Monkey Glands" (*Isle of Hope near Savannah), 7*bib.*

"Mr. Colborne's Profanity-Exterminators," later titled "The Don't-Swear Man" (*A. S. Colborne), 7*bib.*

"Mr. Flood's Party," third part of *Hugh G. Flood story, 7*bib. See also Old Mr. Flood*

"Mr. Grover A. Whalen and the Midway" (*dancers at the 1939 World's Fair), 6*bib.*

"Mr. Hunter's Grave" (*George H. Hunter of Staten Island), xxiv, 5*bib.*, 5, 29, 66, 73. *See also Bottom*

Mr. Personality. See Singer, Mark

Sloppy Louie Morino's Restaurant. *See* New York City
Smith, Amanda, 19*bib.*
*Smith, John S. *See* "Santa Claus Smith"
*Smith, Kate. *See* "Home Girl"
Smith, Stephen, 34*bib.*
Smoller, Sanford, xxiv-xxiv, 34*bib.*
Sokolov, Raymond (biographer of Liebling), xxii, 58*bib.*
Some Times in America and a Life in a Year at the New Yorker (Alexander Chancellor), 41*bib.*, 43, 53
Sourcebook of American Literary Journalism, A: Representative Writers in an Emerging Genre (Thomas B. Connery, Ed.), 42*bib.*
Southern Culture (feature on the Southern mule), 10
*Southern Writers. *See* Owen, Guy
Spark, Muriel, 65
"Spism and a Spasm, A" (*Reverend Mr. James Jefferson Davis Hall), xii, xxiv, 4*bib.*, 17; revisions done for 1992 anthology, 15-16
"Sporting Man, A" (*Commodore Dutch). *See* "Tooth, The"
Stafford, Jean. *See* Liebling, Jean Stafford
Steen, Jan (painter), 30
Steig, William, 57
Steinberg, Saul, xii*i*, xxiii, 13, 56, 58*bib*
Stone, I. F., 54
Stonehill, Alexandra (photographer), 58
Stonehill, Judith (Greenwich Village), 47, 58-59*bib.*.
*Stonington, Connecticut. *See* "Dragger Captain I-II"
Story, Richard David, 34*bib.*, 43
"Story Behind Joseph Mitchell." See Washington, Jim
Streep, Meryl. *See* Orlean, Susan
Streitfeld, David, xii, 35*bib.*
"Strike at the Wind" (outdoor drama). *See* Robeson County
Strunsky, Robert, 35*bib.*
Stuart, Maryland (1959 portrait of Mitchell for American Academy of Arts and Sciences), 32
Subtreasury of American Humor, A (1941 anthology), 9*bib.*
Sullivan, Frank, 51
Sullivan, James Henry, 2
*Sunday, Billy, xiii, xxi

Talalay, Kathryn. *See* *Composition in Black and White* (*Philippa Duke Schuyler)
Talese, Gay, 52, 61. *See also Writing Creative Nonfiction*

ABOUT THE AUTHOR

Raised on a farm near Blue Rapids, Kansas, Raymond Rundus graduated from the College of Emporia in 1955 with a major in English and a minor in French. Working as a Graduate Assistant, he earned his M.A. from Wayne State University in Detroit in 1957.

After serving two years in the Seventh Army as a Signal Corps specialist in Germany and now wed to Brigitte Obermeyer of Stuttgart, he began a five-year stint of high school teaching in his native state in January 1960. Called back to his alma mater in 1965 as an instructor of English, then English chair, he completed his Ph.D. degree in English at the University of Nebraska in 1969.

He began his career at Pembroke State University (now the University of North Carolina at Pembroke) as Chair of English in 1970 and retired as Professor of English in December 1996. Named Professor Emeritus the next year, Dr. Rundus is now a planner, consultant, researcher, and writer. A participant in numerous conferences, he has published poetry, essays, and instructional articles on a great variety of topics. He has twice served as President of the "Friends of the Library" at UNCP and is Chair of the Retired Faculty Club. E-mail: *rjrundus@infionline.net*

0-595-28739-5

7579850R00080

Printed in Great Britain
by Amazon.co.uk, Ltd.,
Marston Gate.